THE SUTTA-NIPÂTA

UUID: cdde8aec-4253-11e5-9bad-119a1b5d0361

This ebook was created with StreetLib Write (http://write.streetlib.com) by Simplicissimus Book Farm

Table of contents

INTRODUCTION

THE Collection of Discourses, Sutta-Nipâta, which I have here translated[1], is very remarkable, as there can be no doubt that it contains some remnants of Primitive Buddhism. I consider the greater part of the Mahâvagga, and nearly the whole of the Atthakavagga as very old. I have arrived at this conclusion from two reasons, first from the language, and secondly from the contents.

1. We not only find here what we meet with in other Pâli poetry, the fuller Vedic forms of nouns and verbs in the plural, as avîtatamhâse, panditâse, dhammâse, sitâse, upatthitâse, pavâdiyâse, &c., and karâmase, asmase, sikkhissâmase; the shorter Vedic plurals and the instrumental singular of nouns, as vinikkhayâ, lakkhanâ for vinikkhayâni, lakkhanâni, mantâ, pariññâ, vinayâ, lâbhakamyâ for mantâya, &c.; Vedic infinitives, as vippahâtave, sampayâtave, unnametave; contracted (or sometimes old) forms, as santyâ, gakkâ, duggakkâ, sammukkâ, titthyâ, thiyo, parihîrati for santiyâ, gâtiyâ, sammutiyâ, titthiyâ, itthiyo, parihariyati, by the side of protracted forms, such as âtumânam; but also some unusual (sometimes old) forms and words, as apukkhasi, sagghasi[2] = sakkhissasi, sussam = sunissâmi (Sansk. sroshyâmi), pâva and

1

pâvâ = vadati, pavekkhe = paveseyya, parikissati = parikilissati, vineyya, vikeyya, nikkheyya, pappuyya, = vinayitvâ, &c., datthu = disvâ (S. drishtvâ), atisitvâ = atikkamitvâ, anuvikka = anuviditvâ, paribbasâna = vasamâna, amhanâ (S. asmanâ) = pâsânena, vâkîbhi, katubbhi, rattamahâbhi, ise (vocative), suvâmi = sâmi, maga = miga,

[1. Sir M. Coomâra Swâmy's translation of part of the book has been a great help to me. I hope shortly to publish the Pâli text.

2. C reads pagghasi.]

tumo = so, parovara = parâvara, bhûnahu = bhûtihanaka, upaya, âmagandha, dhona, vyappatha, vyappathi, vevikkhâ, visenibhûta, visenikatvâ, patiseniyanti. Sometimes we meet also with difficult and irregular constructions, and very condensed expressions. All this proves, I think, that these parts of the book are much older than the Suttas in which the language is not only fluent, but of which some verses are even singularly melodious.

2. In the contents of the Suttanipâta we have, I think, an important contribution to the right understanding of Primitive Buddhism, for we see here a picture not of life in monasteries, but of the life of hermits in its first stage. We have before us not the systematizing of the later Buddhist church, but the first germs of a system, the fundamental ideas of which come out

with sufficient clearness. From the Atthakavagga especially it is evident where Buddha takes his stand in opposition to Philosophy (ditthi = darsana).

Indian society at the time of Buddha had two large and distinguished religious sects, Samanas and Brâhmanas. This is apparent from several passages where they are mentioned together; for instance, Vinaya, ed. Oldenberg, II, p. 295; Grimblot, Sept Suttas Pâlis, p. ix, 8 &c., 118 &c., 158 &c., 306 &c., 309; Dhammapada, p. 392; Suttanipâta; vv. 99, 129, 189, 440, 529, 859, 1078; Sabhiyasutta, at the beginning; the Inscriptions of Asoka; Mahâbhâshya, II, 4, 9 (fol. 398 a); Lalita Vistara, pp. 309, l. 10, 318, l. 18, 320, l. 20; and lastly, Megasthenes (Schwanbeck, p. 45), {Greek: dúo génh figodófwn, wn toùs mèn Braxmanas kalei, toùs dè Sarmanas}.

Famous teachers arose and gathered around them flocks of disciples. As such are mentioned Pûrana-Kassapa, Makkhali-Gosâla, Agita-Kesakarnbali, Pakudha-Kakkâyana, Sañgaya-Belatthiputta, and Nigantha-Nâtaputta[1]; see Suttanipâta, p. 86; Mahâparinibbânasutta, ed. Childers, p. 58; Vinaya II, p. 111; Grimblot, Sept Suttas Pâlis, p. 114, &c.; Milindapañha, ed. Trenckner, p. 4. Besides these there is Bâvari (Suttanipâta, p. 184), and his disciples Agita, Tissametteyya, Punnaka, Mettagû, Dhotaka, Upasîva, Nanda,

[1. Cf. Indian Antiquary, 1880, p. 158.]

3

Hemaka, Todeyya, Kappa, Gatukannin, Bhadrâvudha, Udaya, Posâla, Mogharâgan (Pingiya, vv. 1006-1008; Sela, p. 98), and, Kankin, Târukkha, Pokkharasâti, Gânussoni, Vâsettha, and Bhâradvâga, p. 109.

We learn that there were four kinds of Samanas, viz. Maggaginas, Maggadesakas (or Maggadesins, Maggagghâyins), Maggagîvins, and Maggadûsins, vv. 83-88. Among these Samanas disputes arose, vv. 828, 883-884; a number of philosophical systems were formed, and at the time of Buddha there were as many as sixty-three of them, v. 538. These systems are generally designated by ditthi, vv. 54, 151, 786, 837, 851, &c.; or by ditthigata, vv. 834, 836, 913; or by ditthasuta, v. 778; or by dittha, suta, and muta, vv. 793, 813, 914; or by dittha, suta, sîlavata[1], and muta, vv. 790, 797-798, 836, 887, 1080. The doctrines themselves are called ditthinivesa, v. 785; or nivesana, vv. 209, 470, 801, 846; or vinikkhaya, vv. 838, 866, 887, 894; and he who entertains any of them, is called nivissavâdin, vv. 910, 913.

What is said of the Samanas seems mostly to hold good about the Brâhmanas also. They too are called disputatious, vâdasîla, v. 381, &c., p. 109; and three kinds of them are mentioned, viz. Titthiyas, Âgîvikas, and Niganthas, vv. 380, 891-892. In contradistinction to the Samanas the Brâhmanas are designated as Teviggas, vv. 594, 1019; they are Padakas, Veyyâkaranas, and perfect in Gappa, Nighandu, Ketubha, Itihâsa, &c., v. 595, p. 98. They are called friends of the hymns, v. 139; well versed in the hymns, v. 976; and their principal hymn is Sâvitti[2], vv. 568, 456. They worship and make offerings to the fire, pp. 74, 20. In Brâhmanadhammikasutta the ancient and just Brâhmanas are described in opposition to the later

[1. I am not sure whether sîlavata is to be understood as one notion or two. It is generally written in one word, but at p. 109 Vâsettha says, when one is virtuous and endowed with works, he is a Brâhmana, yato kho bho sîlavâ ka hoti vatasampanno ka ettâvatâ kho brâhmano hoti. Sîlavata, I presume, refers chiefly to the Brâhmanas.

2. From v. 456 we see that Buddha has rightly read vareniyam as the metre requires; but I must not omit to mention that the Commentator understands by Sâvitti the Buddhistic formula: Buddham saranam gakkhâmi, Dhammam saranam gakkhâmi, Samgham saranam gakkhâmi, which, like Sâvitti, contains twenty-four syllables.]

Brâhmanas, who slay innocent cows and have acquired wealth through the favour of the kings. vv. 307, 308, 311, 302[1].

All these disputants hold fast to their own prejudiced views, v. 910. They say that purity comes from philosophical views, from tradition, and from virtuous works, and in many other ways, v. 1078, and that there is no bliss excepting by following their opinions, vv. 889, 891, 892.

Buddha himself has, it is true, sprung from the Samanas: he is called Samana Gotama, p. 96; he shines like a sun in the midst of the Samanas, v. 550; and intercourse with Samanas is said to be the highest blessing, v. 265. But Buddha has overcome all their systems, v. 538; there is nothing which has not been seen, heard, or thought by him, and nothing which has not been understood by him, v. 1121. All the disputatious Brâhmanas do not overcome him in understanding, v. 380; and he asserts that no one is purified and saved by philosophy or by virtuous works, vv. 1079, 839. Sanctification, in fact, does not come from another, vv. 773, 790, 813; it can be attained only by going into the yoke with Buddha, v. 834; by believing in him and in the Dhamma of the Saints, vv. 183, 185, 370, 1142; on the whole, by being what Buddha is.

What then is Buddha?

First he is a Visionary, in the good sense of the word; his knowledge is intuitive. 'Seeing misery,' he says, 'in the philosophical views, without adopting any of them, searching for truth, I saw inward peace,' vv. 837, 207. And again, 'He, a conqueror unconquered, saw the Dhamma visibly, without any traditional instruction,' vv. 934, 1052, 1065. He teaches an instantaneous, an immediate religious life, vv. 567, 1136. He is called kakkhumat, endowed with an eye, clearly-seeing, vv. 160, 405, 540, 562, 596, 956, 992, 1028, 1115, 1127; samantakakkhu, the all-seeing, vv. 1062, 1068; and as such he has become an eye to the world, v. 599. He sees the subtle meaning of things, vv. 376,

175; he is, in one word, Sambuddha, the perfectly-enlightened, vv. 177, 555, 596, 992; and by knowledge he is delivered, vv. 1106,

[1. Besides the religious Brâhmanas some secular Brâhmanas are mentioned, p. 11.]

727, 733. Existence is aviggâ, ignorance, v. 729; viggâ, knowledge, is the extinction of the world, v. 730.

Secondly, he is an Ascetic, a Muni[1], one that forsakes othe world and wanders from the house to the houseless state, vv. 273, 375, 1003; because from house-life arises defilement, v. 206. An ascetic has no prejudiced ideas, v. 802; he has shaken off every philosophical view, v. 787; he does not enter into disputes, v. 887; he is not pleased nor displeased with anything, v. 813; he is indifferent to learning, v. 911; he does not cling to good and evil, vv. 520, 547, 790; he has cut off all passion and all desire, vv. 2, 795, 1130, 916; he is free from marks, v. 847; and possessionless, akiñkana, vv. 175, 454, 490, 620, 1058, 1062, 976, 1069, 1114. He is equable, v. 855; under all circumstances the same, v. 952; still as the deep water, v. 920; calm, vv. 459, 861. He has reached peace, vv. 837, 845, 919; he knows that bliss consists in peace, v. 933; he has gone to immortal peace, the unchangeable state of Nibbâna, v. 203. And how is this state brought about? By the destruction of consciousness, vv. 734-735. And how does consciousness cease? By the cessation of sensation, vv. 1109-1110; by being without breathing, vv. 1089-1090[2].

1. What then is sin according to Buddha?

Subjectively sin is desire, in all its various forms, vv. 923, 1103; viz. desire tor existence generally, vv. 776, 1059, 1067, and especially for name and form, i.e. individual existence, vv. 354, 1099. As long as man is led by desire he will be whirled about in existence, v. 740; for as long as there is birth, there will be death, v. 742. Existence is called the stream of death, v. 354; the realm of Mâra, vv. 164, 1145. Those who continually go to samsâra with birth and death, are the ignorant, v. 729.

[1. Buddha is sometimes styled the great Isi, vv. 1060, 1082; sometimes a Muni, vv. 164, 700; sometimes a Brâhmana, v. 1064; sometimes a Bhikkhu, vv. 411, 415; and all these appellations are used synonymously, vv. 283, 284, 1064, 1056, 843, 844, 911, 912, 946, 220. Ascetic life is praised throughout the book, especially in the Uraga-, Muni-, Râhula-, Sammâparibbâganiya-, Dhammika-, Nâlaka-, Purâbheda-, Tuvataka-, Attadanda-, and Sâriputta-suttas.

2. This system ends, it will be seen from this, like other ascetic systems, in mysticism.]

But desire originates in the body, vv. 270, 1099; sin lies objectively in embodiment or matter, and consequently the human body is looked upon as a contemptible thing. See

8

Vigayasutta, p. 32.

2. And what is bliss?

Subjectively, it is emancipation from desire by means of the peace that Buddha preaches, vv. 1065-1066, 1069, 1084, 1108, 838-839.

Objectively, it is emancipation from body and matter. One must destroy the elements of existence, upadhî, vv. 373, 546, 1050, 1056; and leave the body behind, that one may not come to exist again, vv. 1120, 1122, 761. The ignorant only create upadhî, v. 1050, and go again and again to samsâra, v. 729. The wise do not enter time, kappa, vv. 521, 535, 860; they look upon the world as void, v. 1118; hold that there is nothing really existing, v. 1069; and those whose minds are disgusted with a future existence, the wise who have destroyed their seeds (of existence), go out like a lamp, vv. 234, 353-354. As a flame, blown about by the violence of the wind, goes out, and cannot be reckoned (as existing), even so a Muni, delivered from name and body, disappears, and cannot be reckoned (as existing), v. 1073. For him who has disappeared, there is no form; that by which they say he is, exists for him no longer, v. 1075.

'Exert thyself, then, O Dhotaka,'--so said Bhagavat,--'being wise and thoughtful in this world, let one, having listened to my utterance, learn his own extinction,' v. 1061.

9

Tena h' âtappam karohi,--Dhotakâ 'ti Bhagavâ,--
idh' eva nipako sato
ito sutvâna nigghosam
sikkhe nibbânam attano.

With this short sketch of the contents of the Suttanipâta for a guide, I trust it will be easy to understand even the more obscure parts of the book.

I. URAGAVAGGA.

1. URAGASUTTA.

The Bhikkhu who discards all human passions is compared to a snake that casts his skin.--Text and translation in Fr. Spiegel's Anecdota Pâlica.

1. He who restrains his anger when it has arisen, as (they) by medicines (restrain) the poison of the snake spreading (in the body), that Bhikkhu leaves this and the further shore, as a snake (quits its) old worn out skin. (1)

2. He who has cut off passion entirely, as (they cut off) the lotus-flower growing in a lake, after diving (into the water), that Bhikkhu leaves this and the further shore, as a snake (quits its) old worn out skin. (2)

3. He who has cut off desire entirely, the flowing, the quickly running, after drying it up, that Bhikkhu leaves this and the further shore, as a snake (quits its) old worn out skin. (3)

4. He who has destroyed arrogance entirely, as the flood (destroys) a very frail bridge of reeds, that Bhikkhu leaves this and the further shore, as a snake (quits its) old worn out skin. (4)

5. He who has not found any essence in the existences, like one that looks for flowers on fig-trees, that Bhikkhu leaves this and the further shore, as a snake (quits its) old worn out skin. (5)

p. 2

6. He in whose breast there are no feelings of anger, who has thus overcome reiterated existence, that Bhikkhu leaves this and the further shore, as a snake (quits its) old worn out skin. (6)

7. He whose doubts are scattered, cut off entirely inwardly, that Bhikkhu leaves this and the further shore, as a snake (quits its) old worn out skin. (7)

8. He who did not go too fast forward, nor was left behind, who overcame all this (world of) delusion, that Bhikkhu leaves this and the further shore, as a snake (quits its) old worn out skin. (8)

9. He who did not go too fast forward, nor was left behind, having seen that all this in the world is false, that Bhikkhu leaves this and the further shore, as a snake (quits its) old worn out skin. (9)

10. He who did not go too fast forward, nor was left behind, being free from covetousness, (seeing) that all this is false, that Bhikkhu leaves this and the further shore, as a snake (quits its) old worn out skin. (10)

11. He who did not go too fast forward, nor was left behind, being free from passion, (seeing) that all this is false, that Bhikkhu leaves this and the further shore, as a snake (quits its) old worn out skin. (11)

12. He who did not go too fast forward, nor was left behind, being free from hatred, (seeing) that all this is false, that Bhikkhu leaves this and the further shore, as a snake (quits its) old worn out skin. (12)

13. He who did not go too fast forward, nor was left behind, being free from folly, (seeing) that all this is false, that Bhikkhu leaves his and the further shore, as a snake (quits its) old worn out skin. (13)

p. 3

14. He to whom there are no affections whatsoever, whose sins are extirpated from the root, that Bhikkhu leaves this and the

further shore, as a snake (quits its) old worn out skin. (14)

15. He to whom there are no (sins) whatsoever originating in fear, which are the causes of coming back to this shore, that Bhikkhu leaves this and the further shore, as a snake (quits its) old worn out skin. (15)

16. He to whom there are no (sins) whatsoever originating in desire, which are the causes of binding (men) to existence, that Bhikkhu leaves this and the further shore, as a snake (quits its) old worn out skin. (16)

17. He who, having left the five obstacles, is free from suffering, has overcome doubt, and is without pain, that Bhikkhu leaves this and the further shore. as a snake (quits its) old worn out skin. (17)

Uragasutta is ended.

2. DHANIYASUTTA.

A dialogue between the rich herdsman Dhaniya and Buddha, the one rejoicing in his worldly security and the other in his religious belief.--This beautiful dialogue calls to mind the parable in the Gospel of S. Luke xii.16.

1. 'I have boiled (my) rice, I have milked (my cows),'--so said the

herdsman Dhaniya,--'I am living together with my fellows near the banks of the Mahî (river), (my) house is covered, the fire is kindled: therefore, if thou like, rain, O sky!' (18)

2. 'I am free from anger, free from stubbornness,'--so said Bhagavat,--'I am abiding for one night near the banks of the Mahî (river), my house

p. 4

is uncovered, the fire (of passions) is extinguished: therefore, if thou like, rain, O sky!' (19)

3. 'Gad-flies are not to be found (with me),'--so said the herdsman Dhaniya,--'in meadows abounding with grass the cows are roaming, and they can endure rain when it comes: therefore, if thou like, rain, O sky!' (20)

4. '(By me) is made a well-constructed raft,'--so said Bhagavat,-- 'I have passed over (to Nibbâna), I have reached the further bank, having overcome the torrent (of passions); there is no (further) use for a raft: therefore, if thou like, rain, O sky!' (21)

5. 'My wife is obedient, not wanton,'--so said the herdsman Dhaniya,--'for a long time she has been living together (with

me), she is winning, and I hear nothing wicked of her: therefore, if thou like, rain, O sky!' (22)

6. 'My mind is obedient, delivered (from all worldliness),'--so said Bhagavat,--'it has for a long time been highly cultivated and well-subdued, there is no longer anything wicked in me: therefore, if thou like, rain, O sky!' (23)

7. 'I support myself by my own earnings,'--so said the herdsman Dhaniya,--'and my children are (all) about me, healthy; I hear nothing wicked of them: therefore, if thou like, rain, O sky!' (24)

8. 'I am no one's servant,'--so said Bhagavat,--'with what I have gained I wander about in all the world, there is no need (for me) to serve: therefore, if thou like, rain, O sky!' (25)

9. 'I have cows, I have calves,'-- so said the herdsman Dhaniya;--'I have cows in calf and heifers, and I have also a bull as lord over the cows: therefore, if thou like, rain, O sky!' (26)

10. 'I have no cows, I have no calves,'--so said Bhagavat,--'I have no cows in calf and no heifers, and I have no bull as a lord over the cows: therefore, if thou like, rain, O sky! (27)

11. 'The stakes are driven in, and cannot be shaken,'--so said the

herdsman Dhaniya,--'the ropes are made of muñga grass, new and well-made, the cows will not be able to break them: therefore, if thou like, rain, O sky!' (28)

12. 'Having, like a bull, rent the bonds; having, like an elephant, broken through the galukkhi creeper, I shall not again enter into a womb: therefore, if thou like, rain, O sky!' (29)

Then at once a shower poured down, filling both sea and land. Hearing the sky raining, Dhaniya spoke thus:

13. 'No small gain indeed (has accrued) to us since we have seen Bhagavat; we take refuge in thee, O (thou who art) endowed with the eye (of wisdom); be thou our master, O great Muni!' (30)

14. 'Both my wife and myself are obedient; (if) we lead a holy life before Sugata, we shall conquer birth and death, and put an end to pain.' (31)

15. 'He who has sons has delight in sons,'--so said the wicked Mâra,--'he who has cows has delight likewise in cows; for upadhi (substance) is the delight of man, but he who has no upadhi has no delight.' (32)

16. 'He who has sons has care with (his) sons,'--so said Bhagavat,--'he who has cows has likewise care with (his) cows; for upadhi (is the cause of) people's cares, but he who has no upadhi has no care.' (33)

Dhaniyasutta is ended.

3. KHAGGA VISÂNASUTTA.

Family life and intercourse with others should be avoided, for society has all vices in its train; therefore one should leave the corrupted state of society and lead a solitary life.

1. Having laid aside the rod against all beings, and not hurting any of them, let no one wish for a son, much less for a companion, let him wander alone like a rhinoceros[1]. (34)

2. In him who has intercourse (with others) affections arise, (and then) the pain which follows affection; considering the misery that originates in affection let one wander alone like a rhinoceros. (35)

3. He who has compassion on his friends and confidential (companions) loses (his own) advantage, having a fettered mind; seeing this danger in friendship let one wander alone like a rhinoceros. (36)

4. Just as a large bamboo tree (with its branches) entangled (in each other, such is) the care one has with children and wife; (but) like the shoot of a bamboo not clinging (to anything) let one wander alone like a rhinoceros[2]. (37)

5. As a beast unbound in the forest goes feeding at pleasure, so let the wise man, considering (only his) own will, wander alone like a rhinoceros. (38)

6. There is (a constant) calling in the midst of company, both when sitting, standing, walking, and going away; (but) let one, looking (only) for freedom from desire and for following his own will, wander alone like a rhinoceros. (39)

7. There is sport and amusement in the midst of

[1. Comp Dhp. v. 142.

2. Comp. Dhp. v. 345.]

p. 7

company, and for children there is great affection; (although) disliking separation from his dear friends, let one wander alone like a rhinoceros. (40)

8. He who is at home in (all) the four regions and is not hostile (to any one), being content with this or that, overcoming (all) dangers fearlessly, let him wander alone like a rhinoceros. (41)

9. Discontented are some pabbagitas (ascetics), also some gahatthas (householders) dwelling in houses; let one, caring little about other people's children, wander alone like a rhinoceros. (42)

10. Removing the marks of a gihin (a householder) like a Kovilâra tree whose leaves are fallen, let one, after cutting off heroically the ties of a gihin, wander alone like a rhinoceros. (43)

11. If one acquires a clever companion, an associate righteous and wise, let him, overcoming all dangers, wander about with him glad and, thoughtful[1]. (44)

12. If one does not acquire a clever companion, an associate righteous and wise, then as a king abandoning (his) conquered kingdom, let him wander alone like a rhinoceros[2]. (45)

13. Surely we ought to praise the good luck of having companions, the best (and such as are our) equals ought to be

sought for; not having acquired such friends let one, enjoying (only) allowable things, wander alone like a rhinoceros[3]. (46)

14. Seeing bright golden (bracelets), well-wrought by the goldsmith, striking (against each other when there are) two on one arm, let one wander alone like a rhinoceros. (47)

[1. Comp. Dhp. v. 328.

2. Comp. Dhp. v. 329.

3. Comp. Dhp. v. 61.]

p. 8

15. Thus (if I join myself) with another I shall swear or scold; considering this danger in future, let one wander alone like a rhinoceros. (48)

16. The sensual pleasures indeed, which are various, sweet, and charming, under their different shapes agitate the mind; seeing the misery (originating) in sensual pleasures, let one wander alone like a rhinoceros. (49)

17. These (pleasures are) to me calamities, boils, misfortunes, diseases, sharp pains, and dangers; seeing this danger (originating) in sensual pleasures, let one wander alone like a rhinoceros. (50)

18. Both cold and heat, hunger and thirst, wind and a burning sun, and gad-flies and snakes--having overcome all these things, let one wander alone like a rhinoceros[1]. (51)

19. As the elephant, the strong, the spotted, the large, after leaving the herd walks at pleasure in the forest, even so let one wander alone like a rhinoceros. (52)

20. For him who delights in intercourse (with others, even) that is inconvenient which tends to temporary deliverance; reflecting on the words of (Buddha) the kinsman of the Âdikka family, let one wander alone like a rhinoceros. (53)

21. The harshness of the (philosophical) views I have overcome, I have acquired self-command, I have attained to the way (leading to perfection), I am in possession of knowledge, and not to be led by others; so speaking, let one wander alone like a rhinoceros. (54)

22. Without covetousness, without deceit, without

[1. Comp. Gâtaka I p. 93.]

p. 9

craving, without detraction, having got rid of passions and folly, being free from desire in all the world, let one wander alone like a rhinoceros. (55)

23. Let one avoid a wicked companion who teaches what is useless and has gone into what is wrong, let him not cultivate (the society of) one who is devoted (to and) lost in sensual pleasures, let one wander alone like a rhinoceros. (56)

24. Let one cultivate (the society of) a friend who is learned and keeps the Dhamma, who is magnanimous and wise; knowing the meaning (of things and) subduing his doubts, let one wander alone like a rhinoceros. (57)

25. Not adorning himself, not looking out for sport, amusement, and the delight of pleasure in the world, (on the contrary) being loath of a life of dressing, speaking the truth, let one wander alone like a rhinoceros. (58)

26. Having left son and wife, father and mother, wealth, and

corn, and relatives, the different objects of desire, let one wander alone like a rhinoceros. (59)

27. 'This is a tie, in this there is little happiness, little enjoyment, but more of pain, this is a fish-hook,' so having understood, let a thoughtful man wander alone like a rhinoceros. (60)

28: Having torn the ties, having broken the net as a fish in the water, being like a fire not returning to the burnt place, let one wander alone like a rhinoceros. (61)

29. With downcast eyes, and not prying[1], with his senses guarded, with his mind protected free from

[1. Na ka pâdalolo ti ekassa dutiyo dvinnam tatiyo ti evam ganamaggham pavisitukâmatâya kandûyamânapâdo viya abhavanto dîghakârika-anavatthakârikavirato vâ. Commentator.]

p. 10

passion, not burning (with lust), let one wander alone like a rhinoceros. (62)

30. Removing the characteristics of a gihin (householder), like a

24

Pârikhatta tree whose leaves are cut off, clothed in a yellow robe after wandering away (from his house), let one wander alone like a rhinoceros. (63)

31. Not being greedy of sweet things, not being unsteady, not supporting others, going begging from house to house, having a mind which is not fettered to any household, let one wander alone like a rhinoceros. (64)

32. Having left the five obstacles of the mind, having dispelled all sin, being independent, having cut off the sin of desire, let one wander alone like a rhinoceros. (65)

33. Having thrown behind (himself bodily) pleasure and pain, and previously (mental) joy and distress, having acquired equanimity, tranquillity, purity, let one wander alone like a rhinoceros. (66)

34. Strenuous for obtaining the supreme good (i.e. Nibbâna), with a mind free from attachment, not living in idleness, being firm, endowed with bodily and mental strength, let one wander alone like a rhinoceros. (67)

35. Not abandoning seclusion and meditation, always wandering in (accordance with) the Dhammas[1], seeing misery in the existences, let one wander alone like a rhinoceros[2]. (68)

36. Wishing for the destruction of desire (i.e. Nibbâna), being careful, no fool, learned, strenuous, considerate, restrained, energetic, let one wander alone like a rhinoceros. (69)

[1. Dhammesu nikkam anudhammakarî.

2. Comp. Dhp. v. 20.]

p. 11

37. Like a lion not trembling at noises, like the wind not caught in a net, like a lotus not stained by water, let one wander alone like a rhinoceros. (70)

38. As a lion strong by his teeth, after overcoming (all animals), wanders victorious as the king of the animals, and haunts distant dwelling-places[1], (even so) let one wander alone like a rhinoceros. (71)

39. Cultivating in (due) time kindness, equanimity, compassion, deliverance, and rejoicing (with others), unobstructed by the whole world, let one wander alone like a rhinoceros. (72)

40. Having abandoned both passion and hatred and folly, having rent the ties, not trembling in the loss of life, let one wander alone like a rhinoceros[2]. (73)

41. They cultivate (the society of others) and serve them for the sake of advantage; friends without a motive are now difficult to get, men know their own profit and are impure; (therefore) let one wander alone like a rhinoceros. (74)

Khaggavisânasutta is ended.

4. KASIBHÂRADVÂGASUTTA.

The Brâhmana Kasibhâradvâga reproaches Gotama with idleness, but the latter convinces him that he (Buddha) also works, and so the Brâhmana is converted, and finally becomes a saint. Compare Sp. Hardy, A Manual of Buddhism, p. 214; Gospel of S. John v. 17.
So it was heard by me:

At one time Bhagavat dwelt in Magadha at Dakkhinâgiri in the Brâmana village Ekanalâ. And at that time the Brâmana Kasibhâradvâga's five hundred

[1. Pantânîti dûrâni senâsanânîti vasatitthânâni. Commentator.

p. 12

ploughs were tied (to the yokes) in the sowing season. Then Bhagavat, in the morning, having put on his raiment and taken his bowl and robes, went to the place where the Brâmana Kasibhâradvâga's work (was going on). At that time the Brâmana Kasibhâradvâga's distribution of food took place. Then Bhagavat went to the place where the distribution of food took place, and having gone there, he stood apart. The Brâmana Kasibhâradvâga saw Bhagavat standing there to get alms, and having seen him, he said this to Bhagavat:

'I, O Samana, both plough and sow, and having ploughed and sown, I eat; thou also, O Samana, shouldst plough and sow, and having ploughed and sown, thou shouldst eat.'

'I also, O Brâmana, both plough and sow, and having ploughed and sown, I eat,' so said Bhagavat.

'Yet we do not see the yoke, or the plough, or the ploughshare, or the goad, or the oxen of the venerable Gotama.'

And then the venerable Gotama spoke in this way:

'I also, O Brâmana, both plough and sow, and having ploughed and sown, I eat,' so said Bhagavat.

Then the Brâmana Kasibhâradvâga addressed Bhagavat in a stanza:

1. 'Thou professest to be a ploughman, and yet we do not see thy ploughing; asked about (thy) ploughing, tell us (of it), that we may know thy ploughing.' (75)

2. Bhagavat answered: 'Faith is the seed, penance the rain, understanding my yoke and plough, modesty the pole of the plough, mind the tie, thoughtfulness my ploughshare and goad. (76)

3. 'I am guarded in respect of the body, I am

p. 13

guarded in respect of speech, temperate in food; I make truth to cut away (weeds), tenderness is my deliverance. (77)

4. 'Exertion is my beast of burden; carrying (me) to Nibbâna he goes without turning back to the place where having gone one does not grieve. (78)

5. 'So this ploughing is ploughed, it bears the fruit of immortality; having ploughed this ploughing one is freed from all pain.' (79)

Then the Brâmana Kasibhâradvâga, having poured rice-milk into a golden bowl, offered it to Bhagavat, saying, 'Let the venerable Bhagavat eat of the rice-milk; the venerable is a ploughman, for the venerable Gotama ploughs a ploughing that bears the fruit of immortality.'

6. Bhagavat said: 'What is acquired by reciting stanzas is not to be eaten by me; this is, O Brâmana, not the Dhamma of those that see rightly; Buddha rejects what is acquired by reciting stanzas, this is the conduct (of Buddhas) as long as the Dhamma exists. (80)

7. 'One who is an accomplished great Isi, whose passions are destroyed and whose misbehaviour has ceased, thou shouldst serve with other food and drink, for this is the field for one who looks for good works[1].' (81)

'To whom then, O Gotama, shall I give this rice-milk?' so said

Kasibhâradvâga.

'I do not see, O Brâmana, in the world (of men)

[1. Aññena ka kevalinam mahesim
Khînâsavam kukkukkavûpasantam
Annena pânena upatthahassu,
Khettam hi tam puññapekhassa hoti.
Cf. Sundarikabhâradvâga v. 28.]

p. 14

and gods and Mâras and Brahmans, amongst beings comprising gods and men, and Samanas and Brâmanas, any by whom this rice-milk when eaten can be properly digested with the exception of Tathâgata, or a disciple of Tathâgata. Therefore, O Brâmana, thou shalt throw this rice-milk in (a place where there is) little grass, or cast it into water with no worms: so said Bhagavat.

Then the Brâmana Kasibhâradvâga threw the rice-milk into some water with no worms. Then the rice-milk thrown into the water splashed, hissed, smoked in volumes; for as a ploughshare that has got hot during the day when thrown into the water splashes, hisses, and smokes in volumes, even so the rice-milk (when) thrown into the water splashed, hissed, and smoked in volumes.

Then the Brâmana Kasibhâradvâga alarmed and terrified went up to Bhagavat, and after having approached and fallen with his head at Bhagavat's feet, he said this to Bhagavat:

'It is excellent, O venerable Gotama! It is excellent, O venerable Gotama! As one raises what has been overthrown, or reveals what has been hidden, or tells the way to him who has gone astray, or holds out an oil lamp in the dark that those who have eyes may see the objects, even so by the venerable Gotama in manifold ways the Dhamma (has been) illustrated. I take refuge in the venerable Gotama and in the Dhamma and in the Assembly of Bhikkhus; I wish to receive the pabbaggâ, I wish to receive the upasampadâ (the robe and the orders) from the venerable Gotama,' so said Kasibhâradvâga.

Then the Brâmana Kasibhâradvâga received the

p. 15

pabbaggâ from Bhagavat, and he received also the upasampadâ; and the venerable Bhâradvâaga having lately received the upasampadâ, leading a solitary, retired, strenuous, ardent, energetic life, lived after having in a short time in this existence by his own understanding ascertained and possessed himself of that highest perfection of a religious life for the sake

32

of which men of good family rightly wander, away from their houses to houseless state. 'Birth had been destroyed, a religious life had been led, what was to be done had been done, there was nothing else (to be done) for this existence,' so he perceived, and the venerable Bhâradvâaga became one of the arahats (saints).

Kasibhâradvâgasutta is ended.

5. KUNDASUTTA.

Buddha describes the four different kinds of Samanas to Kunda, the smith.

1. 'I ask the Muni of great understanding,'--so said Kunda, the smith,--'Buddha, the lord of the Dhamma, who is free from desire, the best of bipeds, the most excellent of charioteers, how many (kinds of) Samanas are there in the world; pray tell me that?' (82)

2. 'There are four (kinds of) Samanas, (there is) not a fifth, O Kunda,'--so said Bhagavat,--'these I will reveal to thee, being asked in person; (they are) Maggaginas and Maggadesakas, Maggagîvins and Maggadûsins.' (83)

3. 'Whom do the Buddhas call a Maggagina?'--so said Kunda, the smith,--'How is a Maggagghâyin

unequalled? Being asked, describe to me a Maggagîvin, and reveal to me a Maggadûsin.' (84)

4. Bhagavat said: 'He who has overcome doubt, is without pain, delights in Nibbâna, is free from greed, a leader of the world of men and gods, such a one the Buddhas call a maggagina (that is, victorious by the way). (85)

5. 'He who in this world having known the best (i.e. Nibbâna) as the best, expounds and explains here the Dhamma, him, the doubt-cutting Muni, without desire, the second of the Bhikkhus they call a maggadesin (that is, teaching the way). (86)

6. 'He who lives in the way that has so well been taught in the Dhammapada, and is restrained, attentive, cultivating blameless words, him the third of the Bhikshus they call a maggagîvin (that is, living in the way[1]). (87)

7. 'He who although counterfeiting the virtuous is forward, disgraces families, is impudent, deceitful, unrestrained, a babbler, walking in disguise, such a one is a maggadûsin (that is, defiling the way)[2]. (88)

8. 'He who has penetrated these (four Samanas), who is a householder, possessed of knowledge, a pupil of the venerable ones, wise, having known that they all are such,--having seen so, his faith is not lost; for how could he make the undepraved equal to the depraved and the pure equal to the impure?' (89)

Kundasutta is ended.

[1. Yo Dhammapade sudesite
Magge gîvati saññato satîmâ
Anavaggapadâni sevamâno
Tatiyam bhikkhunam âhu maggagîvim.

2. Comp. Gâtaka II, p. 281.]

p. 17

6. PARÂBHAVASUTTA.

A dialogue between a deity and Buddha on the things by which a man loses and those by which he gains in this world.--Text by Grimblot, in Journal Asiatique, t. xviii (1871), p. 237; translation by L. Feer, in Journal Asiatique, t. xviii (1871), p. 309, and by Gogerly, reprinted in Journal Asiatique, t. xx (1872), p. 226.

So it was heard by me:

At one time Bhagavat dwelt at Sâvatthî, in Getavana, in the park of Anâthapindika. Then when the night had gone, a certain deity of a beautiful appearance, having illuminated the whole Getavana, went up to Bhagavat, and having approached and saluted him, he stood apart, and standing apart that deity addressed Bhagavat in stanzas:

1. 'We ask (thee), Gotama, about a man that suffers loss; having come to ask, Bhagavat, (tell us) what is the cause (of loss) to the losing (man).' (90)

2. Bhagavat: 'The winner is easily known, easily known (is also) the loser: he who loves Dhamma is the winner, he who hates Dhamma is the loser.' (91)

3. Deity: 'We know this to be so, this is the first loser; tell (us) the second, O Bhagavat, what is the cause (of loss) to the losing (man).' (92)

4. Bhagavat: 'Wicked men are dear to him, he does not do anything that is dear to the good, he approves of the Dhamma of the wicked,--that is the cause (of loss) to the losing (man).' (93)

5. Deity: 'We know this to be so, this is the second loser; tell us the third, O Bhagavat, what is the cause (of loss) to the losing (man).' (94)

6. Bhagavat: 'The man who is drowsy, fond of society and without energy, lazy, given to anger,--that is the cause (of loss) to the losing (man).' (95)

p. 18

7. Deity: 'We know this to be so, this is the third loser; tell us the fourth, O Bhagavat, what is the cause (of loss) to the losing (man).' (96)

8. Bhagavat: 'He who being rich does not support mother or father who are old or past their youth,--that is the cause (of loss) to the losing (man).' (97)

9. Deity: 'We know this to be so, this is the fourth loser; tell us the fifth, O Bhagavat, what is the cause (of loss) to the losing (man).' (98)

10. Bhagavat: 'He who by falsehood deceives either a Brâmana or a Samana or any other mendicant,--that is the cause (of loss) to the losing (man).' (99)

11. Deity: 'We know this to be so, this is the fifth loser; tell us the sixth, O Bhagavat, what is the cause (of loss) to the losing (man).' (100)

12. Bhagavat: 'The man who is possessed of much property, who has gold and food, (and still) enjoys alone his sweet things,--that is the cause (of loss) to the losing (man).' (101)

13. Deity: 'We know this to be so, this is the sixth loser; tell us the seventh, O Bhagavat, what is the cause (of loss) to the losing (man).' (102)

14. Bhagavat: 'The man who proud of his birth, of his wealth, and of his family, despises his relatives,--that is the cause (of loss) to the losing (man).' (103)

15. Deity: 'We know this to be so, this is the seventh loser; tell us the eighth, O Bhagavat, what is the cause (of loss) to the losing (man).' (104)

16. Bhagavat: 'The man who given to women, to strong drink, and to dice, wastes whatever he has gained,--that is the cause (of loss) to the losing (man).' (105)

17. Deity: 'We know this to be so, this is the eighth loser; tell us the ninth, O Bhagavat, what is the cause (of loss) to the losing (man).' (106)

18. Bhagavat: 'He who, not satisfied with his own wife, is seen with harlots and the wives of others,--that is the cause (of loss) to the losing (man).' (107)

19. Deity: 'We know this to be so, this is the ninth loser; tell us the tenth, O Bhagavat, what (is) the cause (of loss) to the losing (man).' (108)

20. Bhagavat: 'The man who, past his youth, brings home a woman with breasts like the timbaru fruit, and for jealousy of her cannot sleep,--that is the cause (of loss) to the losing (man).' (109)

21. Deity: 'We know this to be so, this is the tenth loser; tell us the eleventh, O Bhagavat, what is the cause (of loss) to the losing (man).' (110)

22. Bhagavat: 'He who places in supremacy a woman given to drink and squandering, or a man of the same kind,--that is the

cause (of loss) to the losing (man).' (111)

23. Deity: 'We know this to be so, this is the eleventh loser; tell us the twelfth, O Bhagavat, what is the cause (of loss) to the losing (man).' (112)

24. Bhagavat: 'He who has little property, (but) great desire, is born in a Khattiya family and wishes for the kingdom in this world,--that is the cause (of loss) to the losing (man).' (113)

25. Having taken into consideration these losses in the world, the wise, venerable man, who is endowed with insight, cultivates the happy world (of the gods).' (114)

Parâbhavasutta is ended.

p. 20

7. VASALASUTTA.

The Brâmana Aggikabhâradvâga is converted by Buddha, after hearing his definition of an outcast, illustrated by the story of Mâtanga, told in the Mâtangagâtaka. Comp. Sp. Hardy, The Legends and Theories of the Buddhists, p. 49.--Text and translation in Alwis's Buddhist Nirvâna, p. 119.

So it was heard by me: At one time Bhagavat dwelt at Sâvatthî, in Getavana, in the park of Anâthapindika. Then Bhagavat having put on his raiment in the morning, and having taken his bowl and his robes, entered Sâvatthî for alms. Now at that time in the house of the Brâmana Aggikabhâradvâga the fire was blazing, the offering brought forth. Then Bhagavat going for alms from house to house in Sâvatthî went to the house of the Brâmana Aggikabhâradvâga. The Brâmana Aggikabhâradvâga saw Bhagavat coming at a distance, and seeing him he said this: 'Stay there, O Shaveling; (stay) there, O Samanaka (i.e. wretched Samana); (stay) there, O Vasalaka (i.e. outcast)!'

This having been said, Bhagavat replied to the Brâmana Aggikabhâradvâga: 'Dost thou know, O Brâmana, an outcast, or the things that make an outcast?'

'No, O venerable Gotama, I do not know an outcast, or the things that make an outcast; let the venerable Gotama teach me this so well that I may know an outcast, or the things that make an outcast."

'Listen then, O Brâmana, attend carefully, I will tell (thee).'

'Even so, O venerable one,' so the Brâmana Aggikabhâradvâga replied to Bhagavat.

Then Bhagavat said this:

1. 'The man who is angry and bears hatred, who is wicked and hypocritical, who has embraced wrong views, who is deceitful, let one know him as an outcast. (115)

2. 'Whosoever in this world harms living beings, whether once or twice born, and in whom there is no compassion for living beings, let one know him as an outcast. (116)

3. 'Whosoever destroys or lays siege to villages and towns, and is known as an enemy, let one know him as an outcast. (117)

4. 'Be it in the village or in the wood, whosoever appropriates by theft what is the property of others and what has not been given, let one know him as an outcast. (118)

5. 'Whosoever, having really contracted a debt, runs away when called upon (to pay), saying, "There is no debt (that I owe) thee," let one know him as an outcast. (119)

6. 'Whosoever for love of a trifle having killed a man going along the road, takes the trifle, let one know him as an outcast.

(120)

7. 'The man who for his own sake or for that of others or for the sake of wealth speaks falsely when asked as a witness, let one know him as an outcast. (121)

8. 'Whosoever is seen with the wives of relatives or of friends either by force or with their consent, let one know him as an outcast. (122)

9. 'Whosoever being rich does not support mother or father when old and past their youth, let one know him as an outcast. (123)

10. 'Whosoever strikes or by words annoys mother

p. 22

or father, brother, sister, or mother-in-law, let one know him as an outcast. (124)

11. 'Whosoever, being asked about what is good, teaches what is bad and advises (another, while) concealing (something from him), let one know him as an outcast. (125)

12. 'Whosoever, having committed a bad deed, hopes (saying), "Let no one know me" (as having done it, who is) a dissembler, let one know him as an outcast. (126)

13. 'Whosoever, having gone to another's house and partaken of his good food, does not in return honour him when he comes, let one know him as an outcast. (127)

14. 'Whosoever by falsehood deceives either a Brâhmana or a Samana or any other mendicant, let one know him as an outcast. (128)

15. 'Whosoever by words annoys either a Brâhmana or a Samana when meal-time has come and does not give (him anything), let one know him as an outcast. (129)

16. 'Whosoever enveloped in ignorance in this world predicts what is not (to take place), coveting a trifle, let one know him as an outcast. (130)

17. 'Whosoever exalts himself and despises others, being mean by his pride, let one know him as an outcast. (131)

18. 'Whosoever is a provoker and is avaricious, has sinful

desires, is envious, wicked, shameless, and fearless of sinning, let one know him as an outcast. (132)

19. 'Whosoever reviles Buddha or his disciple, be he a wandering mendicant (paribbâga) or a householder (gahattha), let one know him as an outcast. (133)

p. 23

20. 'Whosoever without being a saint (arahat) pretends to be a saint, (and is) a thief in all the worlds including that of Brahman, he is indeed the lowest outcast; (all) these who have been described by me to you are indeed called outcasts. (134)

21. 'Not by birth does one become an outcast, not by birth does one become a Brâmana; by deeds one becomes an outcast, by deeds one becomes a Brâmana. (135)

22. 'Know ye this in the way that this example of mine (shows): There was a Kandâla of the Sopâka caste, well known as Mâtanga. (136)

23. 'This Mâtanga reached the highest fame, such as was very difficult to obtain, and many Khattiyas and Brâmanas went to serve him. (137)

24. 'He having mounted the vehicle of the gods, (and entered) the high road (that is) free from dust, having abandoned sensual desires, went to the Brahma world. (138)

25. 'His birth did not prevent him from being re-born in the Brahma world; (on the other hand) there are Brâmanas, born in the family of preceptors, friends of the hymns (of the Vedas), (139)

26. 'But they are continually caught in sinful deeds, and are to be blamed in this world, while in the coming (world) hell (awaits them); birth does not save them from hell nor from blame. (140)

27. '(Therefore) not by birth does one become an outcast, not by birth does one become a Brâmana, by deeds one becomes an outcast, by deeds one becomes a Brâmana.' (141)

This having been said, the Brâmana Aggikabhâradvâga answered Bhagavat as follows:

'Excellent, O venerable Gotama! Excellent, O

venerable Gotama! As one, O venerable Gotama, raises what has been overthrown, or reveals what has been hidden, or tells the way to him who has gone astray, or holds out an oil lamp in the dark that those who have eyes may see the objects, even so by the venerable Gotama in manifold ways the Dhamma has been illustrated; I take refuge in the venerable Gotama and in the Dhamma and in the Assembly of Bhikkhus. Let the venerable Gotama accept me as an upâsaka (a follower, me) who henceforth for all my life have taken refuge (in him).'

Vasalasutta is ended.

8. METTASUTTA.

A peaceful mind and goodwill towards all beings are praised.-- Text by Grimblot in Journal Asiatique, t. xviii (1871), p. 250, and by Childers in Khuddaka Pâtha, p. 15; translation (?) by Gogerly in the Ceylon Friend, 1839, p. 211, by Childers in Kh. Pâtha and by L. Feer in Journal Asiatique, t. xviii (1871), p. 328.

1. Whatever is to be done by one who is skilful in seeking (what is) good, having attained that tranquil state (of Nibbâna):--Let him be able and upright and conscientious and of soft speech, gentle, not proud, (142)

2. And contented and easily supported and having few cares,

unburdened and with his senses calmed and wise, not arrogant, without (showing) greediness (when going his round) in families. (143)

3. And let him not do anything mean for which others who are wise might reprove (him); may all beings be happy and secure, may they be happy-minded. (144)

p. 25

4. Whatever living beings there are, either feeble or strong, all either long or great, middle-sized, short, small or large, (145)

5. Either seen or which are not seen, and which live far (or) near, either born or seeking birth, may all creatures be happy-minded. (146)

6. Let no one deceive another, let him not despise (another) in any place, let him not out of anger or resentment wish harm to another. (147)

7. As a mother at the risk of her life watches over her own child, her only child, so also let every one cultivate a boundless (friendly) mind towards all beings. (148)

8. And let him cultivate goodwill towards all the world, a boundless (friendly) mind, above and below and across, unobstructed, without hatred, without enmity. (149)

9. Standing, walking or sitting or lying, as long as he be awake, let him devote himself to this mind; this (way of) living they say is the best in this world. (150)

10. He who, not having embraced (philosophical) views, is virtuous, endowed with (perfect) vision, after subduing greediness for sensual pleasures, will never again go to a mother's womb. (151)

Mettasutta is ended.

9. HEMAVATASUTTA.

A dialogue between two Yakkhas on the qualities of Buddha. They go to Buddha, and after having their questions answered they, together with ten hundred Yakkhas, become the followers of Buddha.

1. 'To-day is the fifteenth, a fast day; a lovely

p. 26

49

night has come,'--so said the Yakkha Sâtâgira,--'let us (go and) see the renowned Master Gotama.' (152)

2. 'Is the mind of such a one well disposed towards all beings?'-- so said the Yakkha Hemavata,--'are his thoughts restrained as to things wished for or not wished for?' (153)

3. 'His mind is well disposed towards all beings, (the mind) of such a one,'--so said the Yakkha Sâtâgira,--'and his thoughts are restrained as to things wished for or not wished for.' (154)

4. 'Does he not take what has not been given (to him)?'--so said the Yakkha Hemavata,--'is he self-controlled (in his behaviour) to living beings? is he far from (a state of) carelessness? does he not abandon meditation?' (155)

5. 'He does not take what has not been given (to him),'--so said the Yakkha Sâtâgira,--'and he is self-controlled (in his behaviour) to living beings, and he is far from (a state of) carelessness; Buddha does not abandon meditation.' (156)

6. 'Does he not speak falsely?'--so said the Yakkha Hemavata,-- 'is he not harsh-spoken? does he not utter slander? does he not talk nonsense?' (157)

7. 'He does not speak falsely,'--so said the Yakkha Sâtâgira,--'he is not harsh-spoken, he does not utter slander, with judgment he utters what is good sense.' (158)

8. 'Is he not given to sensual pleasures?'--so said the Yakkha Hemavata,--'is his mind undisturbed? has he overcome folly? does he see clearly in (all) things (dhammas)?' (159)

9. 'He is not given to sensual pleasures,'--so said the Yakkha Sâtâgira,--'and his mind is undisturbed;

p. 27

he has overcome all folly; Buddha sees clearly in (all) things.' (160)

10. 'Is he endowed with knowledge?'--so said the Yakkha Hemavata,--'is his conduct pure? have his passions been destroyed? is there no new birth (for him)?' (161)

11. 'He is endowed with knowledge,'--so said the Yakkha Sâtâgira,--'and his conduct is pure; all his passions have been destroyed; there is no new birth for him. (162)

12. 'The mind of the Muni is accomplished in deed and word; Gotama, who is accomplished by his knowledge and conduct, let us (go and) see. (163)

13. 'Come, let us (go and) see Gotama, who has legs like an antelope, who is thin, who is wise, living on little food, not covetous, the Muni who is meditating in the forest. (164)

14. 'Having gone to him who is a lion amongst those that wander alone and does not look for sensual pleasures, let us ask about the (means of) deliverance from the snares of death. (165)

15. 'Let us ask Gotama, the preacher, the expounder, who has penetrated all things, Buddha who has overcome hatred and fear.' (166)

16. 'In what has the world originated?'--so said the Yakkha Hemavata,--'with what is the world intimate? by what is the world afflicted, after having grasped at what?' (167)

17. 'In six the world has originated, O Hemavata,'--so said Bhagavat,--'with six it is intimate, by six the world is afflicted, after having grasped at six.' (168)

18. Hemavata said: 'What is the grasping by

which the world is afflicted? Asked about salvation, tell (me) how one is released from pain?' (169)

19. Bhagavat said: 'Five pleasures of sense are said to be in the world, with (the pleasure of) the mind as the sixth; having divested oneself of desire for these, one is thus released from pain. (170)

20. 'This salvation of the world has been told to you truly, this I tell you: thus one is released from pain.' (171)

21. Hemavata said: 'Who in this world crosses the stream (of existence)? who in this world crosses the sea? who does not sink into the deep, where there is no footing and no support?' (172)

22. Bhagavat said: 'He who is always endowed with virtue, possessed of understanding, well composed, reflecting within himself, and thoughtful, crosses the stream that is difficult to cross. (173)

23. 'He who is disgusted with sensual pleasures, who has overcome all bonds and destroyed joy, such a one does not sink

into the deep.' (174)

24. Hemavata said: 'He who is endowed with a profound understanding, seeing what is subtile, possessing nothing, not clinging to sensual pleasures, behold him who is in every respect liberated, the great Isi, walking in the divine path. (175)

25. 'He who has got a great name, sees what is subtile, imparts understanding; and does not cling to the abode of sensual pleasures, behold him, the all-knowing, the wise, the great Isi, walking in the noble path. (176)

26. 'A good sight indeed (has met) us to-day, a good daybreak, a beautiful rising, (for) we have seen the perfectly enlightened (sambuddham), who has crossed the stream, and is free from passion. (177)

p. 29

27. 'These ten hundred Yakkhas, possessed of supernatural power and of fame, they all take refuge in thee, thou art our incomparable Master. (178)

28. 'We will wander about from village to village, from mountain to mountain, worshipping the perfectly enlightened and the perfection of the Dhamma[1].' (179)

Hemavatasutta is ended.

10. ÂLAVAKASUTTA.

The Yakkha Âlavaka first threatens Buddha, then puts some questions to him which Buddha answers, whereupon Âlavaka is converted.

So it was heard by me:

At one time Bhagavat dwelt at Âlavî, in the realm of the Yakkha Âlavaka. Then the Yakkha Âlavaka went to the place where Bhagavat dwelt, and having gone there he said this to Bhagavat:

'Come out, O Samana!'

'Yes, O friend!' so saying Bhagavat came out.

'Enter, O Samana!'

'Yes, O friend!' so saying Bhagavat entered.

A second time the Yakkha Âlavaka said this to Bhagavat: 'Come out, O Samana!'

'Yes, O friend!' so saying Bhagavat came out.

'Enter, O Samana!'

'Yes, O friend!' so saying Bhagavat entered.

A third time the Yakkha Âlavaka said this Bhagavat: 'Come out, O Samana!'

' Yes, O friend!' so saying Bhagavat came out.

'Enter, O Samana!'

[1. Dhammassa ka sudhammatam.]

p. 30

'Yes, O friend!' so saying Bhagavat entered.

A fourth time the Yakkha Âlavaka said this to Bhagavat: 'Come out, O Samana!'

'I shall not come out to thee, O friend, do what thou pleasest.'

'I shall ask thee a question, O Samana, if thou canst not answer it, I will either scatter thy thoughts or cleave thy heart, or take thee by thy feet and throw thee over to the other shore of the Gangâ.'

'I do not see, O friend, any one in this world nor in the world of gods, Mâras, Brahmans, amongst the beings comprising gods, men, Samanas, and Brâhmanas, who can either scatter my thoughts or cleave my heart, or take me by the feet and throw me over to the other shore of the Gangâ; however, O friend, ask what thou pleasest.'

Then the Yakkha Âlavaka addressed Bhagavat in stanzas:

1. 'What in this world is the best property for a man? what, being well done, conveys happiness? what is indeed the sweetest of sweet things? how lived do they call life the best?' (180)

2. Bhagavat said: 'Faith is in this world the best property for a man; Dhamma, well observed, conveys happiness; truth indeed

is the sweetest of things; and that life they call the best which is lived with understanding.' (181)

3. Âlavaka said: 'How does one cross the stream (of existence)? how does one cross the sea? how does one conquer pain? how is one purified?' (182)

4. Bhagavat said: 'By faith one crosses the stream, by zeal the sea, by exertion one conquers pain, by understanding one is purified.' (183)

p. 31

5. Âlavaka said: 'How does one obtain understanding? how does one acquire wealth? how does one obtain fame? how does one bind friends (to himself)? how does one not grieve passing away from this world to the other?' (184)

6. Bhagavat said: 'He who believes in the Dhamma of the venerable ones as to the acquisition of Nibbâna, will obtain understanding from his desire to hear, being zealous and discerning. (185)

7. 'He who does what is proper, who takes the yoke (upon him and) exerts himself, will acquire wealth, by truth he will obtain fame, and being charitable he will bind friends (to himself).

(186)

8. 'He who is faithful and leads the life of a householder, and possesses the following four Dhammas (virtues), truth, justice (dhamma), firmness, and liberality,--such a one indeed does not grieve when passing away. (187)

9. 'Pray, ask also other Samanas and Brâhmanas far and wide, whether there is found in this world anything greater than truth, self-restraint, liberality, and forbearance.' (188)

10. Âlavaka said: 'Why should I now ask Samanas and Brâhmanas far and wide? I now know what is my future good. (189)

11. 'For my good Buddha came to live at Âlavî; now I know where (i.e. on whom bestowed) a gift will bear great fruit. (190)

12. 'I will wander about from village to village, from town to town, worshipping the perfectly enlightened (sambuddha) and the perfection of the Dhamma.' (191)

Âlavakasutta is ended.

11. VIGAYASUTTA.

A reflection on the worthlessness of the human body; a follower of Buddha only sees the body as it really is, and consequently goes to Nibbâna.--Comp. Gâtaka I, p. 146.

1. If either walking or standing, sitting or lying, any one contracts (or) stretches (his body, then) this is the motion of the body. (192)

2. The body which is put together with bones and sinews, plastered with membrane and flesh, and covered with skin, is not seen as it really is. (193)

3. It is filled with the intestines, the stomach, the lump of the liver, the abdomen, the heart, the lungs, the kidneys, the spleen. (194)

4. With mucus, saliva, perspiration, lymph, blood, the fluid that lubricates the joints, bile, and fat. (195)

5. Then in nine streams impurity flows always from it; from the eye the eye-excrement, from the ear the ear-excrement, (196)

6. Mucus from the nose, through the mouth it ejects at one time bile and (at other times) it ejects phlegm, and from (all) the

body come sweat and dirt. (197)

7. Then its hollow head is filled with the brain. A fool led by ignorance thinks it a fine thing. (198)

8. And when it lies dead, swollen and livid, discarded in the cemetery, relatives do not care (for it). (199)

9. Dogs eat it and jackals, wolves and worms; crows and vultures eat it, and what other living creatures there are. (200)

10. The Bhikkhu possessed of understanding in this world, having listened to Buddha's words, he

p. 33

certainly knows it (i.e. the body) thoroughly, for he sees it as it really is. (201)

11. "As this (living body is) so is that (dead one), as this is so that (will be[1]); let one put away desire for the body, both as to its interior and as to its exterior." (202)

12. Such a Bhikkhu who has turned away from desire and attachment, and is possessed of understanding in this world, has (already) gone to the immortal peace, the unchangeable state of Nibbâna. (203)

13. This (body) with two feet is cherished (although) impure, ill-smelling, filled with various kinds of stench, and trickling here and there. (204)

14. He who with such a body thinks to exalt himself or despises others--what else (is this) but blindness? (205)

Vigayasutta is ended.

12. MUNISUTTA.

Definition of a Muni.
1. From acquaintanceship arises fear, from house-life arises defilement; the houseless state, freedom from acquaintanceship--this is indeed the view of a Muni. (206)

2. Whosoever, after cutting down the (sin that has) arisen, does not let (it again) take root and does not give way to it while springing up towards him, him

[1. Yathâ idam tathâ etam
Yathâ etam tathâ idam.]

the solitarily wandering they call a Muni; such a great Isi has
seen the state of peace[1]. (207)

3. Having considered the causes (of sin, and) killed the seed, let
him not give way to desire for it; such a Muni who sees the end
of birth and destruction (i.e. Nibbâna), after leaving reasoning
behind, does not enter the number (of living beings)[2]. (208)

4. He who has penetrated all the resting-places[3] (of the mind,
and) does not wish for any of them,--such a Muni indeed, free
from covetousness and free from greediness, does not gather
up (resting-places), for he has reached the other shore. (209)

5. The man who has overcome everything, who knows
everything, who is possessed of a good understanding,
undefiled in all things (dhamma), abandoning everything,
liberated in the destruction of desire (i.e. Nibbâna), him the wise
style a Muni[4]. (210)

6. The man who has the strength of understanding, is endowed
with virtue and (holy) works, is composed, delights in
meditation, is thoughtful, free from ties, free from harshness
(akhila), and free from passion, him the wise style a Muni. (211)

7. The Muni that wanders solitarily, the zealous,

[1. Yo gâtam ukkhigga na ropayeyya
Gâyantam assa nânuppavekkhe
Tam âhu ekam muninam karantam,
Addakkhi so santipadam mahesi.

2. Samkhâya vatthûni pamâya bîgam
Sineham assa nânuppavekkhe,
Sa ve munî gâtikhayantadassî
Takkam pahâya na upeti samkham.

3. Nivesanâni. Comp. Dutthaka, v. 6.

4. Comp. Dhp. v. 353.]

that is not shaken by blame and praise, like a lion not trembling at noises, like the wind not caught in a net, like a lotus not soiled by water, leading others, not led by others, him the wise style a Muni. (212)

8. Whosoever becomes firm as the post in a bathing-place, in whom others acknowledge propriety of speech, who is free from passion, and (endowed) with well-composed senses, such a one the wise style a Muni. (213)

9. Whosoever is firm, like a straight shuttle, and is disgusted with evil actions, reflecting on what is just and unjust, him the wise style a Muni. (214)

10. Whosoever is self-restrained and does not do evil, is a young or middle-aged Muni, self-subdued, one that should not be provoked (as) he does not provoke any, him the wise style a Muni. (215)

11. Whosoever, living upon what is given by others, receives a lump of rice from the top, from the middle or from the rest (of the vessel, and) does not praise (the giver) nor speak harsh words, him the wise style a Muni. (216)

12. The Muni that wanders about abstaining from sexual intercourse, who in his youth is not fettered in any case, is abstaining from the insanity of pride, liberated, him the wise style a Muni. (217)

13. The man who, having penetrated the world, sees the highest truth, such a one, after crossing the stream and sea (of existence), who has cut off all ties, is independent, free from passion, him indeed the wise style a Muni. (218)

14. Two whose mode of life and occupation are quite different, are not equal: a householder maintaining a wife, and an unselfish virtuous man. A householder (is intent) upon the destruction of other living creatures, being unrestrained; but a Muni always protects living creatures, being restrained. (219)

15. As the crested bird with the blue neck (the peacock) never attains the swiftness of the swan, even so a householder does not equal a Bhikkhu, a secluded Muni meditating in the wood. (220)

Munisutta is ended.

Uragavagga is ended.

II. KÛLAVAGGA.

1. RATANASUTTA.

For all beings salvation is only to be found in Buddha, Dhamma, and Sangha.--Text and translation in Childers' Khuddaka Pâtha, p. 6.

1. Whatever spirits have come together here, either belonging to the earth or living in the air, let all spirits be happy, and then listen attentively to what is said. (221)

2. Therefore, O spirits, do ye all pay attention, show kindness to the human race who both day and night bring their offerings; therefore protect them strenuously. (222)

3. Whatever wealth there be here or in the other world, or whatever excellent jewel in the heavens, it is certainly not equal to Tathâgata. This excellent jewel (is found) in Buddha, by this truth may there be salvation. (223)

4. The destruction (of passion), the freedom from passion, the

excellent immortality which Sakyamuni attained (being) composed,--there is nothing equal to that Dhamma. This excellent jewel (is found) in the Dhamma, by this truth may there be salvation. (224)

5. The purity which the best of Buddhas praised, the meditation which they call uninterrupted, there is no meditation like this. This excellent jewel (is

p. 38

found) in the Dhamma, by this truth may there be salvation. (225)

6. The eight persons that are praised by the righteous[1], and make these four pairs, they are worthy of offerings, (being) Sugata's disciples; what is given to these will bear great fruit. This excellent jewel (is found) in the Assembly (sangha), by this truth may there be salvation. (226)

7. Those who have applied themselves studiously with a firm mind and free from desire to the commandments of Gotama, have obtained the highest gain, having merged into immortality, and enjoying happiness after getting it for nothing. This excellent jewel (is found) in the Assembly, by this truth may there be salvation. (227)

8. As a post in the front of a city gate is firm in the earth and cannot be shaken by the four winds, like that I declare the righteous man to be who, having penetrated the noble truths, sees (them clearly). This excellent jewel (is found) in the Assembly, by this truth may there be salvation. (228)

9. Those who understand the noble truths well taught by the profoundly wise (i.e. Buddha), though they be greatly distracted, will not (have to) take the eighth birth. This excellent jewel (is found) in the Assembly, by this truth may there be salvation. (229)

10. On his (attaining the) bliss of (the right) view three things (dhammas) are left behind (by him): conceit and doubt and whatever he has got of virtue and (holy) works. He is released also from the four hells, and he is incapable of committing the six

[1. The Commentator: satam pasatthâ ti sappurisehi buddhapakkekabuddhasâvakehi aññehi ka devamanusehi pasatthâ.]

p. 39

deadly sins. This excellent jewel (is found) in the Assembly, by

69

this truth may there be salvation. (230)

11. Even if he commit a sinful deed by his body, or in word or in thought, he is incapable of concealing it, (for) to conceal is said to be impossible for one that has seen the state (of Nibbâna). This excellent jewel (is found) in the Assembly, by this truth may there be salvation. (231)

12. As in a clump of trees with their tops in bloom in the first heat of the hot month, so (Buddha) taught the excellent Dhamma leading to Nibbâna to the greatest benefit (for all). This excellent jewel (is found) in Buddha, by this truth may there be salvation. (232)

13. The excellent one who knows what is excellent, who gives what is excellent, and who brings what is excellent, the incomparable one taught the excellent Dhamma. This excellent jewel (is found) in Buddha, by this truth may there be salvation. (233)

14. The old is destroyed, the new has not arisen, those whose minds are disgusted with a future existence, the wise who have destroyed their seeds (of existence, and) whose desires do not increase, go out like this lamp. This excellent jewel (is found) in the Assembly, by this truth may there be salvation. (234)

15. Whatever spirits have come together here, either belonging

to the earth or living in the air, let us worship the perfect (tathâgata) Buddha, revered by gods and men; may there be salvation. (235)

16. Whatever spirits have come together here, either belonging to the earth or living in the air, let us worship the perfect (tathâgata) Dhamma, revered by gods and men; may there be salvatlon. (236)

17. Whatever spirits have come together here,

p. 40

either belonging to the earth or living in the air, let us worship the perfect (tathâgata) Sangha, revered by gods and men; may there be salvation. (237)

Ratanasutta is ended.

2. ÂMAGANDHASUTTA.

A bad mind and wicked deeds are what defiles a man; no outward observances can purify him. Comp. Gospel of S. Matthew xv. 10.

1. Âmagandhabrâhmana: 'Those who eat sâmâka, kingûlaka, and kînaka, pattaphala, mûlaphala, and gaviphala (different sorts of grass, leaves, roots, &c.), justly obtained of the just, do not speak falsehood, (nor are they) desirous of sensual pleasures. (238)

2. 'He who eats what has been well prepared, well dressed, what is pure and excellent, given by others, he who enjoys food made of rice, eats, O Kassapa, Âmagandha (what defiles one). (239)

3. '(The charge of) Âmagandha does not apply to me,' so thou sayest, 'O Brahman (brahmabandhu, although) enjoying food (made) of rice together with the well-prepared flesh of birds. I ask thee, O Kassapa, the meaning of this, of what description (is then) thy Âmagandha?' (240)

4. Kassapabuddha: 'Destroying living beings, killing, cutting, binding, stealing, speaking falsehood, fraud and deception, worthless reading[1], intercourse with another's wife;--this is Âmagandha, but not the eating of flesh. (241)

[1.   Agghenakuggan   ti niratthakânatthaganakaganthapariyâpunanam. Commentator.]

p. 41

5. 'Those persons who in this world are unrestrained in (enjoying) sensual pleasures, greedy of sweet things, associated with what is impure, sceptics (natthikaditthi), unjust, difficult to follow;--this is Âmagandha, but not the eating of flesh. (242)

6. 'Those who are rough, harsh, backbiting, treacherous, merciless, arrogant, and (who being) illiberal do not give anything to any one;--this is Âmagandha, but not the eating of flesh. (243)

7. 'Anger, intoxication, obstinacy, bigotry, deceit, envy, grandiloquence, pride and conceit, intimacy with the unjust;--this is Âmagandha, but not the eating of flesh. (244)

8. 'Those who in this world are wicked, and such as do not pay their debts, are slanderers, false in their dealings, counterfeiters, those who in this world being the lowest of men commit sin;--this is Âmagandha, but not the eating of flesh. (245)

9. 'Those persons who in this world are unrestrained (in their behaviour) towards living creatures, who are bent upon injuring after taking others' (goods), wicked, cruel, harsh, disrespectful;--this is Âmagandha, but not the eating of flesh. (246)

10. 'Those creatures who are greedy of these (living beings, who

are) hostile, offending; always bent upon (evil) and therefore, when dead, go to darkness and fall with their heads downwards into hell;--this is Âmagandha, but not the eating of flesh. (247)

11. 'Neither the flesh of fish, nor fasting, nor nakedness, nor tonsure, nor matted hair, nor dirt, nor rough skins, nor the worshipping of the fire, nor the many immortal penances in the world, nor hymns, nor oblations, nor sacrifice, nor observance of the

p. 42

seasons, purify a mortal who has not conquered his doubt[1]. (248)

12. 'The wise man wanders about with his organs of sense guarded, and his senses conquered, standing firm in the Dhamma, delighting in what is right and mild; having overcome all ties and left behind all pain, he does not cling to what is seen and heard.' (249)

13. Thus Bhagavat preached this subject again and again, (and the Brâhmana) who was accomplished in the hymns (of the Vedas) understood it; the Muni who is free from defilement, independent, and difficult to follow, made it clear in various stanzas. (250)

14. Having heard Buddha's well-spoken words, which are free from defilement and send away all pain, he worshipped Tathâgata's (feet) in humility, and took orders at once. (251)

Âmagandhasutta is ended.

3. HIRISUTTA.

On true frendship.
1. He who transgresses and despises modesty, who says, 'I am a friend,' but does not undertake any work that can be done, know (about) him: 'he is not my (friend).' (252)

2. Whosoever uses pleasing words to friends without effect[2], him the wise know as one that (only) talks, but does not do anything. (253)

3. He is not a friend who always eagerly suspects a breach and looks out for faults; but he with whom he dwells as a son at the breast (of his mother),

[1. Comp. Dhp. v. 141.

2. Ananvayan ti yam attham dassâmi karissâmîti bhâsati tena ananugatam. Commentator.]

p. 43

he is indeed a friend that cannot be severed (from him) by others. (254)

4. He who hopes for fruit, cultivates the energy that produces joy and the pleasure that brings praise, (while) carrying the human yoke[1]. (255)

5. Having tasted the sweetness of seclusion and tranquillity one becomes free from fear and free from sin, drinking in the sweetness of the Dhamma[2]. (256)

Hirisutta is ended.

4. MAHÂMANGALASUTTA.

Buddha defines the highest blessing to a deity.--Text by Grimblot in Journal Asiatique, t. xviii (1871), p. 229, and by Childers in Kh. Pâtha, p. 4; translation by Gogerly in the Ceylon Friend, 1839, p. 208; by Childers in Kh. Pâtha, p. 4; and by L. Feer in Journal Asiatique, t. xviii (1871), p. 296.

So it was heard by me:

At one time Bhagavat dwelt at Sâvatthî, in Getavana, in the park of Anâthapindika. Then, when the night had gone, a deity of beautiful appearance, having illuminated the whole Getavana, approached Bhagavat, and having approached and saluted him, he stood apart, and standing apart that deity addressed Bhagavat in a stanza:

1. 'Many gods and men have devised blessings, longing for happiness, tell thou (me) the highest blessing.' (257)

2. Buddha said: 'Not cultivating (the society of)

[1. Pâmuggakaranam thânam
Pasamsâvahanam sukham
Phalânisamso[*] bhâveti
Vahanto porisam dhuram.

2. Comp. Dhp. v. 205.

*. Phalam patikankhamâno phalânisamso. Commentator.]

p. 44

fools, but cultivating (the society of) wise men, worshipping those that are to be worshipped, this is the highest blessing. (258)

3. 'To live in a suitable country, to have done good deeds in a former (existence), and a thorough study of one's self, this is the highest blessing. (259)

4. 'Great learning and skill, well-learnt discipline, and well-spoken words, this is the highest blessing. (260)

5. 'Waiting on mother and father, protecting child and wife, and a quiet calling, this is the highest blessing. (261)

6. 'Giving alms, living religiously, protecting relatives, blameless deeds, this is the highest blessing. (262)

7. 'Ceasing and abstaining from sin, refraining from intoxicating drink, perseverance in the Dhammas, this is the highest blessing. (263)

8. 'Reverence and humility, contentment and gratitude, the hearing of the Dhamma at due seasons, this is the highest blessing. (264)

9. 'Patience and pleasant speech, intercourse with Samanas, religious conversation at due seasons, this is the highest blessing. (265)

10. 'Penance and chastity, discernment of the noble truths, and the realisation of Nibbâna, this is the highest blessing. (266)

11. 'He whose mind is not shaken (when he is) touched by the things of the world (lokadhamma), (but remains) free from sorrow, free from defilement, and secure, this is the highest blessing. (267)

12. 'Those who, having done such (things), are undefeated in every respect, walk in safety everywhere, theirs is the highest blessing.' (268)

Mahâmangala is ended.

p. 45

5. SÛKILOMASUTTA.

The Yakkha Sûkiloma threatens to harm Buddha, if he cannot answer his questions. Buddha answers that all passions proceed from the body.

So it was heard by me:

At one time Bhagavat dwelt at Gayâ (seated) on a stone seat in the realm of the Yakkha Sûkiloma. And at that time the Yakkha Khara and the Yakkha Sûkiloma passed by, not far from Bhagavat. And then the Yakkha Khara said this to the Yakkha Sûkiloma: 'Is this man a Samana?'

Sûkiloma answered: 'He is no Samana, he is a Samanaka (a wretched Samana); however I will ascertain whether he is a Samana or a Samanaka.'

Then the Yakkha Sûkiloma went up to Bhagavat, and having gone up to him, he brushed against Bhagavat's body. Then Bhagavat took away his body. Then the Yakkha Sûkiloma said this to Bhagavat: 'O Samana, art thou afraid of me?'

Bhagavat answered: 'No, friend, I am not afraid of thee, but thy touching me is sinful.'

Sûkiloma said: 'I will ask thee a question, O Samana; if thou canst not answer it I will either scatter thy thoughts or cleave thy heart, or take thee by the feet and throw thee over to the other shore of the Gangâ.'

80

Bhagavat answered: 'I do not see, O friend, neither in this world together with the world of the Devas, Mâras, Brahmans, nor amongst the generation of Samana and Brâhmanas, gods and men, the one who can either scatter my thoughts or cleave my heart, or take me by the feet and throw me over

p. 46

to the other shore of the Gangâ. However ask, O friend, what thou pleasest.' Then the Yakkha Sûkiloma addressed Bhagavat in a stanza:

1. ' What origin have passion and hatred, disgust, delight, and horror? wherefrom do they arise? whence arising do doubts vex the mind, as boys vex a crow?' (269)

2. Buddha said: 'Passion and hatred have their origin from this (body), disgust, delight, and horror arise from this body; arising from this (body) doubts vex the mind, as boys vex a crow. (270)

3. 'They originate in desire, they arise in self, like the shoots of the banyan tree; far and wide they are connected, with sensual pleasures, like the mâluvâ creeper spread in the wood. (271)

4. 'Those who know whence it (sin) arises, drive it away. Listen, O Yakkha! They cross over this stream that is difficult to cross, and has not been crossed before, with a view to not being born again.' (272)

Sûkilomasutta is ended.

6. DHAMMAKARIYASUTTA OR KAPILASUTTA.

The Bhikkhus are admonished to rid themselves of sinful persons and advised to lead a pure life.
1. A just life, a religious life, this they call the best gem, if any one has gone forth from house-life to a houseless life. (273)

2. But if he be harsh-spoken, and like a beast delighting in injuring (others), then the life of such a one is very wicked, and he increases his own pollution. (274)

p. 47

3. A Bhikkhu who delights in quarrelling and is shrouded in folly, does not understand the Dhamma that is preached and taught by Buddha. (275)

4. Injuring his own cultivated mind, and led by ignorance, he does not understand that sin is the way leading to hell. (276)

5. Having gone to calamity, from womb to womb, from darkness to darkness, such a Bhikkhu verily, after passing away, goes to pain. (277)

6. As when there is a pit of excrement (that has become) full during a number of years,--he who should be such a one full of sin is difficult to purify. (278)

7. Whom you know to be such a one, O Bhikkhus, (a man) dependent on a house, having sinful desires, sinful thoughts, and being with sinful deeds and objects, (279)

8. Him do avoid, being all in concord; blow him away as sweepings, put him away as rubbish. (280)

9. Then remove as chaff those that are no Samanas, (but only) think themselves, blowing away those that have sinful desires and those with sinful deeds and objects. (281)

10. Be pure and live together with the pure, being thoughtful; then agreeing (and) wise you will put an end to pain. (282)

Dhammakariyasutta is ended.

7. BRÂHMANADMAMMIKASUTTA.

Wealthy Brâhmanas come to Buddha, asking about the customs of the ancient Brâhmanas. Buddha describes their mode of life and the change wrought in them by seeing the king's riches, and furthermore, how they induced the king to commit the sin of
p. 48

having living creatures slain at sacrifices. On hearing Buddha's enlightened discourse the wealthy Brâhmanas are converted. Compare Sp. Hardy's Legends, p. 46.
So it was heard by me:

At one time Bhagavat dwelt at Sâvatthî, in Getavana, in the park of Anâthapindika. Then many wealthy Brâhmanas of Kosala, decrepit, elderly, old, advanced in age, or arrived at extreme old age, went to Bhagavat, and having gone to him they talked pleasantly with him, and after having had some pleasant and remarkable talk with him, they sat down apart. Sitting down apart these wealthy Brâhmanas said this to Bhagavat: 'O venerable Gotama, are the Brâhmanas now-a-days seen (engaged) in the Brâhmanical customs (dhamma) of the ancient Brâhmanas?'

Bhagavat answered: 'The Brâhmanas now-a-days, O Brâhmanas, are not seen (engaged) in the Brâhmanical customs of the ancient Brâhmanas.'

The Brâhmanas said: 'Let the venerable Gotama tell us the Brâhmanical customs of the ancient Brâhmanas, if it is not inconvenient to the venerable Gotama.'

Bhagavat answered: 'Then listen, O Brâhmanas, pay great attention, I will speak.'

'Yes,' so saying the wealthy Brâhmanas listened to Bhagavat. Bhagavat said this:

1. The old sages (isayo) were self-restrained, penitent; having abandoned the objects of the five senses, they studied their own welfare. (283)

2. There were no cattle for the Brâhmanas, nor gold, nor corn, (but) the riches and corn of meditation were for them, and theey kept watch over the best treasure. (284)

p. 49

3. What was prepared for them and placed as food at the door, they thought was to be given to those that seek for what has been prepared by faith. (285)

4. With garments variously coloured, with beds and abodes, prosperous people from the provinces and the whole country worshipped those Brâhmanas. (286)

5. Inviolable were the Brâhmanas, invincible, protected by the Dhamma, no one opposed them (while standing) at the doors of the houses anywhere. (287)

6. For forty-eight years they practised juvenile chastity, the Brâhmanas formerly went in search of science and exemplary conduct. (288)

7. The Brâhmanas did not marry (a woman belonging to) another (caste), nor did they buy a wife; they chose living together in mutual love after having come together. (289)

8. Excepting from the time about the cessation of the menstruation else the Brâhmanas did not indulge in sexual intercourse[1]. (290)

9. They praised chastity and virtue, rectitude, mildness,

penance, tenderness, compassion, and patience. (291)

10. He who was the best of them, a strong Brâhmana, did not (even) in sleep indulge in sexual intercourse. (292)

11. Imitating his practices some wise men in this world praised chastity and patience. (293)

12. Having asked for rice, beds, garments, butter. and oil, and gathered them justly, they made sacrifices

[1. Aññatra tamhâ samayâ
Utuveramanim pati
Antarâ methunam dhammam
Nâsu gakkhanti brâhmanâ.]

p. 50

out of them, and when the sacrifice came on, they did not kill cows. (294)

13. Like unto a mother, a father, a brother, and other relatives the cows are our best friends, in which medicines are produced. (295)

14. They give food, and they give strength, they likewise give (a good) complexion and happiness; knowing the real state of this, they did not kill cows. (296)

15. They were graceful, large, handsome, renowned, Brâhmanas by nature, zealous for their several works; as long as they lived in the world, this race prospered. (297)

16. But there was a change in them: after gradually seeing the king's prosperity and adorned women, (298)

17. Well-made chariots drawn by noble horses, carpets in variegated colours, palaces and houses, divided into compartments and measured out, (299)

18. The great human wealth, attended with a number of cows, and combined with a flock of beautiful women, the Brâhmanas became covetous. (300)

19. They then, in this matter, having composed hymns, went to Okkâka, and said: 'Thou hast much wealth and corn, sacrifice thy great property, sacrifice thy great wealth.' (301)

20. And then the king, the lord of chariots, instructed by the

Brâhmanas, brought about assamedha, purisamedha, sammâpâsa, and vâkâpeyya without any hinderance, and having offered these sacrifices he gave the Brâhmanas wealth: (302)

21. Cows, beds, garments, and adorned women, and well-made chariots, drawn by noble horses, carpets in variegated colours, (303)

p. 51

22. Beautiful palaces, well divided into compartments; and having filled these with different (sorts of) corn, he gave this wealth to the Brâhmanas. (304)

23. And they having thus received wealth wished for a store, and the desire of those who had given way to (their) wishes increased still more; they then, in this matter, having composed hymns, went again to Okkâka, and said: (305)

24. 'As water, earth, gold, wealth, and corn, even so are there cows for men, for this is a requisite for living beings; sacrifice thy great property, sacrifice thy wealth.' (306)

25. And then the king, the lord of chariots, instructed by the

Brâhmanas, caused many hundred thousand cows to be slain in offerings. (307)

26. The cows, that are like goats, do not hurt any one with their feet or with either of their horns, they are tender, and yield vessels (of milk),--seizing them by the horns the king caused them to be slain with a weapon. (308)

27. Then the gods, the forefathers, Inda, the Asuras, and the Rakkhasas cried out: 'This is injustice,' because of the weapon falling on the cows. (309)

28. There were formerly three diseases: desire, hunger, and decay, but from the slaying of cattle there came ninety-eight. (310)

29. This injustice of (using) violence that has come down (to us), was old; innocent (cows) are slain, the sacrificing (priests) have fallen off from the Dhamma. (311)

30. So this old and mean Dhamma is blamed by the wise; where people see such a one, they blame the sacrificing priest. (312)

p. 52

31. So Dhamma being lost, the Suddas and the Vessikas disagreed, the Khattiyas disagreed in manifold ways, the wife despised her husband. (313)

32. The Khattiyas and the Brâhmanas and those others who had been protected by their castes, after doing away with their disputes on descent, fell into the power of sensual pleasures. (314)

This having been said, those wealthy Brâhmanas said to Bhagavat as follows:

'It is excellent, O venerable Gotama! It is excellent, O venerable Gotama! As one raises what has been overthrown, or reveals what has been hidden, or tells the way to him who has gone astray, or holds out an oil lamp in the dark that those who have eyes may see the objects, even so by the venerable Gotama in manifold ways the Dhamma has been illustrated; we take refuge in the venerable Gotama, in the Dhamma, and in the Assembly of Bhikkhus; may the venerable Gotama receive us as followers (upâsaka), who from this day for life have taken refuge (in him).'

Brâhmanadhammikasutta is ended.

8. NÂVÂSUTTA.

On choosing a good and learned teacher.

1. A man should worship him from whom he learns the Dhamma, as the gods (worship) Inda; the learned man being worshipped and pleased with him, makes the (highest) Dhamma manifest. (315)

2. Having heard and considered that (Dhamma), the wise man practising the Dhamma that is in

p. 53

accordance with the (highest) Dhamma, becomes learned, expert, and skilful, strenuously associating with such a (learned teacher). (316)

3. He who serves a low (teacher), a fool who has not understood the meaning, and who is envious, goes to death, not having overcome doubt, and not having understood the Dhamma. (317)

4. As a man, after descending into a river, a turgid water with a rapid current, is borne along following the current,--how will he be able to put others across? (318)

5. Even so how will a man, not having understood the Dhamma, and not attending to the explanation of the learned and not knowing it himself, not having overcome doubt, be able to make others understand it? (319)

6. As one, having gone on board a strong ship, provided with oars and rudder, carries across in it many others, knowing the way to do it, and being expert and thoughtful, (320)

7. So also he who is accomplished, of a cultivated mind, learned, intrepid, makes others endowed with attention and assiduity understand it, knowing (it himself). (321)

8. Therefore indeed one should cultivate (the society of) a good man, who is intelligent and learned; he who leads a regular life, having understood what is good and penetrated the Dhamma, will obtain happiness. (322)

Nâvâsutta is ended.

p. 54

9. KIMSÎLASUTTA.

How to obtain the highest good.

1. By what virtue, by what conduct, and performing what works, will a man be perfectly established (in the commandments) and obtain the highest good? (323)

2. Let him honour old people, not be envious, let him know the (right) time for seeing his teachers, let him know the (right) moment for listening to their religious discourses, let him assiduously hearken to their well-spoken (words). (324)

3. Let him in due time go to the presence of his teachers, let him be humble after casting away obstinacy, let him remember and practise what is good, the Dhamma, self-restraint, and chastity. (325)

4. Let his pleasure be the Dhamma, let him delight in the Dhamma, let him stand fast in the Dhamma, let him know how to enquire into the Dhamma, let him not raise any dispute that pollutes the Dhamma, and let him spend his time in (speaking) well-spoken truths[1]. (326)

5. Having abandoned ridiculous talk, lamentation, corruption, deceit, hypocrisy, greediness and haughtiness, clamour and harshness, depravity and foolishness, let him live free from infatuation, with a steady mind. (327)

6. The words, the essence of which is understood, are well

spoken, and what is heard, if understood, contains the essence of meditation; but the understanding and learning of the man who is hasty and careless, does not increase. (328)

[1. Comp. Dhp. v. 364.]

p. 55

7. Those who delight in the Dhamma, proclaimed by the venerable ones, are unsurpassed in speech, mind and work, they are established in peace, tenderness and meditation, and have gone to the essence of learning and understanding. (329)

Kimsîlasutta is ended.

10. UTTHÂNASUTTA.

Advice not to be lukewarm and slothful.
1. Rise, sit up, what is the use of your sleeping; to those who are sick, pierced by the arrow (of pain), and suffering, what sleep is there? (330)

2. Rise, sit up, learn steadfastly for the sake of peace, let not the king of death, knowing you to be indolent (pamatta), befool you

and lead you into his power. (331)

3. Conquer this desire which gods and men stand wishing for and are dependent upon, let not the (right) moment pass by you; for those who have let the (right) moment pass, will grieve when they have been consigned to hell. (332)

4. Indolence (pamâda) is defilement, continued indolence is defilement; by earnestness (appamâda) and knowledge let one pull out his arrow. (333)

Utthânasutta is ended.

11. RÂHULASUTTA.

Buddha recommends the life of a recluse to Râhula, and admonishes him to turn his mind away from the world and to be moderate.
1. Bhagavat said: 'Dost thou not despise the wise man, from living with him constantly? Is he

p. 56

who holds up a torch to mankind honoured by thee?' (334)

2. Râhula: 'I do not despise the wise man, from living with him constantly; he who holds up a torch to mankind is always honoured by me.' (335)

Vatthugâthâ.

3. Bhagavat: 'Having abandoned the objects of the five senses, the beautiful, the charming, and gone out from thy house with faith, do thou put an end to pain. (336)

4. 'Cultivate (the society of) virtuous friends and a distant dwelling-place, secluded and quiet; be moderate in food[1]. (337)

5. 'Robes, alms (in bowl), requisites (for the sick), a dwelling-place,--do not thirst after these (things), that thou mayest not go back to the world again. (338)

6. 'Be subdued according to the precepts, and as to the five senses, be attentive as regards thy body, and be full of disgust (with the world). (339)

7. 'Avoid signs, what is pleasant and is accompanied with passion, turn thy mind undisturbed and well composed to what

is not pleasant. (340)

8. 'Cherish what is signless, leave the inclinations for pride; then by destroying pride thou shalt wander calm.' (341)

So Bhagavat repeatedly admomshed the venerable Râhula with these stanzas.

Râhulasutta is ended.

[1. Mitte bhagassu kalyâne
Pantañ ka sayanâsanam
Vivittam appanigghosam,
Mattaññû hohi bhogane.
Comp. Dhp. v. 185 and v. 375.]

p. 57

12. VANGÎSASUTTA.

Vangîsa desires to know the fate of Nigrodhakappa, whether he has been completely extinguished, or whether he is still with some elements of existence left behind. He is answered by Buddha.

So it was heard by me:

At one time Bhagavat dwelt at Alavî, in the temple of Aggâlava. At that time the teacher of the venerable Vangîsa, the Thera, by name Nigrodhakappa, had attained bliss not long before (akiraparinibbuta). Then this reflection occurred to the venerable Vangîsa, while retired and meditating:

Whether my teacher be blessed (parinibbuta) or whether he be not blessed. Then the venerable Vangîsa, at the evening time, coming forth from his retirement went to Bhagavat, and having gone to him he sat down apart after saluting him, and sitting down apart the venerable Vangîsa said this to Bhagavat:

'Lord, while retired and meditating, this reflection occurred to me here: Whether my teacher be blessed or whether he be not blessed.'

Then the venerable Vangîsa, rising from his seat, throwing his robe over one shoulder and bending his joined hands towards Bhagavat, addressed him in stanzas:

1. 'We ask the Master of excellent understanding: he who in this world had cut off doubt, died at Aggâlava, a Bhikkhu, well known, famous, and of a calm mind. (342)

2. 'The name "Nigrodhakappa" was given to that Brâhmana by thee, O Bhagavat; he wandered

p. 58

about worshipping thee, having liberation in view, strong, and seeing Nibbâna. (343)

3. 'O Sakka, thou all-seeing, we all wish to learn (something about) this disciple; our ears are ready to hear, thou art our Master, thou art incomparable. (344)

4. 'Cut off our doubt, tell me of him, inform us of the blessed, O thou of great understanding; speak in the midst of us, O thou all-seeing, as the thousand-eyed Sakka (speaks in the midst) of the gods. (345)

5. 'Whatever ties there are in this world (constituting) the way to folly, combined with ignorance, forming the seat of doubt, they do not exist before Tathâgata, for he is the best eye of men. (346)

6. 'If a man does not for ever dispel the sin as the wind (dispels) a mass of clouds, all the world will be enveloped in darkness, not even illustrious men will shine. (347)

7. 'Wise men are light-bringers, therefore, O wise man, I consider thee as such a one; we have come to him who beholds meditation, reveal Kappa to us in the assembly. (348)

8. 'Uplift quickly, O thou beautiful one, thy beautiful voice, like the swans drawing up (their necks) sing softly with a rich and well-modulated voice; we will all listen to thee attentively. (349)

9. 'Having earnestly called upon him who has completely left birth and death behind and shaken off (sin), I will make him proclaim the Dhamma, for ordinary people cannot do what they want, but the Tathâgatas act with a purpose[1]. (350)

[1. Pahînagâtimaranam asesam
Niggayha dhonam vadessâmi dhammam,
Na kâmakâro hi puthugganânam
Samkheyyakâro ka tathâgatânam.]

p. 59

10. 'This full explanation by thee, the perfectly wise, is accepted, this last clasping of the hands is well bent, O thou of high wisdom, knowing (Kappa's transmigration), do not delude us[1]. (351)

11. ' Having perfectly[2] comprehended the Dhamma of the venerable ones, do not delude (us), O thou of unsurpassed strength, knowing (everything); as one in the hot season pained by the heat (longs for) water, so I long for thy words; send a shower of learning. (352)

12. 'The rich religious life which Kappâyana led, has not that been in vain (to him), has he been (completely) extinguished; or is he still with some elements of existence (left behind)? How he was liberated, that we want to hear.' (353)

13. Bhagavat: 'He cut off the desire for name and form in this world,'--so said Bhagavat,--'Kanha's (i.e. Mâra's) stream, adhered to for a long time, he crossed completely birth and death,' so said Bhagavat, the best of the five (Brâhmanas, pañkavaggiyâ). (354)

14. Vangîsa: 'Having heard thy word, O thou the best of the Isis, I am pleased; not in vain have I asked, the Brâhmana did not deceive me. (355)

15. 'As he talked so he acted, he was a (true) disciple of Buddha, he cut asunder the outspread strong net of deceitful death. (356)

16. 'Kappiya (Kappâyana) saw, O Bhagavat, the beginning

[1. Sampannaveyyâkaranam tava-y-idam
Samuggupaññassa samuggahîtam,
Ayam añgali pakkhimo suppanâmito,
Mâ mohayi gânam anomapañña.

2. Parovaran ti lokuttaralokiyavasena sundarâsundaram dûre santikam vâ. Commentator.]

p. 60

of attachment, Kappâyana verily crossed the realm of death, which is very difficult to cross.' (357)

Vangîsasutta is ended.

13. SAMMÂPARIBBÂGANIYASUTTA.

The right path for a Bhikkhu.
1. 'We will ask the Muni of great understanding, who has crossed, gone to the other shore, is blessed (parinibbuta), and of a firm mind: How does a Bhikkhu wander rightly in the world, after having gone out from his house and driven away desire?' (358)

2. 'He whose (ideas of) omens, meteors, dreams and signs are destroyed,'--so said Bhagavat,--'such a Bhikkhu who has abandoned the sinful omens, wanders rightly in the world. (359)

3. 'Let the Bhikkhu subdue his passion for human and divine pleasures, then after conquering existence and understanding the Dhamma, such a one will wander rightly in the world. (360)

4. 'Let the Bhikkhu, after casting behind him slander and anger, abandon avarice and be free from compliance and opposition, then such a one will wander rightly in the world. (361)

5. 'He who having left behind both what is agreeable and what is disagreeable, not seizing upon anything, is independent in every respect and liberated from bonds, such a one will wander rightly in the world. (362)

6. 'He does not see any essence in the Upadhis, having subdued his wish and passion for attachments,

p. 61

he is independent and not to be led by others, such a one will wander rightly in the world[1]. (363)

7. 'He who is not opposed (to any one) in word, thought or deed, who, after having understood the Dhamma perfectly, longs for the state of Nibbâna, such a one will wander rightly in the world. (364)

8. 'He who thinking "he salutes me" is not elated, the Bhikkhu who, although abused, does not reflect (upon it, and) having received food from others does not get intoxicated (with pride), such a one will wander rightly in the world. (365)

9. 'The Bhikkhu who, after leaving behind covetousness and existence, is disgusted with cutting and binding (others), he who has overcome doubt, and is without pain, such a one will wander rightly in the world. (366)

10. 'And knowing what becomes him, the Bhikkhu will not harm any one in the world, understanding the Dhamma thoroughly, such a one will wander rightly in the world. (367)

11. 'He to whom there are no affections whatsoever, whose sins are extirpated from the root, he free from desire and not longing (for anything), such a one will wander rightly in the world. (368)

12. 'He whose passions have been destroyed, who is free from

pride, who has overcome all the path of passion, is subdued, perfectly happy (parinibbuta), and of a firm mind, such a one will wander rightly in the world. (369)

13. 'The believer, possessed of knowledge, seeing

[1. Na so upadhîsu sâram eti
Âdânesu vineyya khandarâgam
So anissito anaññaneyyo
Sammâ so.]

p. 62

the way (leading to Nibbâna), who is no partisan amongst the partisans (of the sixty-two philosophical views), wise after subduing covetousness, anger, such a one will wander rightly in the world. (370)

14. 'He who is pure and victorious, who has removed the veil (of the world), who is subdued in the Dhammas, has gone to the other shore, is without desire, and skilled in the knowledge of the cessation of the Samkhâras, such a one will wander rightly in the world. (371)

15. 'He who has overcome time (kappâtîta) in the past and in the future, is of an exceedingly pure understanding, liberated from

106

all the dwelling-places (of the mind), such a one will wander rightly in the world. (372)

16. 'Knowing the step (of the four truths), understanding the Dhamma, seeing clearly the abandonment of the passions, destroying all the elements of existence (upadhî), such a one will wander rightly in the world.' (373)

17. 'Certainly, O Bhagavat, it is so: whichever Bhikkhu lives in this way, subdued and having overcome all bonds, such a one will wander rightly in the world.' (374)

Sammâparibbâganiyasutta is ended.

14. DHAMMIKASUTTA.

Buddha shows Dhammika what the life of a Bhikkhu and what the life of a householder ought to be.
So it was heard by me:

At one time Bhagavat dwelt at Sâvatthî, in Getavana, in the park of Anâthapindika. Then the follower (upâsaka) Dhammika, together with five hundred followers, went to Bhagavat, and having gone to Bhagavat and saluted him, he sat down apart; sitting down apart the follower Dhammika addressed Bhagavat in stanzas:

1. 'I ask thee, O Gotama of great understanding, How is a Sâvaka (disciple) to act to be a good one? is it the one who goes from his house to the wilderness, or the followers with a house? (375)

2. 'For thou knowest the doings of this world and that of the gods, and the final end; there is nobody like thee seeing the subtle meaning (of things); they call thee the excellent Buddha. (376)

3. 'Knowing all knowledge thou hast revealed the Dhamma, having compassion on creatures; thou hast removed the veil (of the world), thou art all-seeing, thou shinest spotless in all the world. (377)

4. 'The king of elephants, Erâvana by name, hearing that thou wert Gina (the Conqueror), came to thy presence, and having conversed with thee he went away delighted, after listening (to thee, and saying), "Very good!" (378)

5. 'Also king Vessavana Kuvera came to ask thee about the

Dhamma; him, too, thou, O wise man, answeredst when asked, and he also after listening was delighted. (379)

6. 'All these disputatious Titthiyas and Âgîvikas and Niganthas do not any of them overcome thee in understanding, as a man standing (does not overcome) the one that is walking quickly. (380)

7. 'All these disputatious Brâhmanas, and there are even some old Brâhmanas, all are bound by thy opinion, and others also that are considered disputants. (381)

8. 'This subtle and pleasant Dhamma that has

p. 64

been well proclaimed by thee, O Bhagavat, and which we all long to hear, do thou, O thou best of Buddhas, speak to us when asked. (382)

9. 'Let all these Bhikkhus and also Upâsakas that have sat down to listen, hear the Dhamma learnt (anubuddha) by the stainless (Buddha), as the gods (hear) the well-spoken (words) of Vâsava.' (383)

10. Bhagavat: 'Listen to me, O Bhikkhus, I will teach you the Dhamma that destroys sin, do ye keep it, all of you; let him who looks for what is salutary, the thoughtful, cultivate the mode of life suitable for Pabbagitas. (384)

11. 'Let not the Bhikkhu walk about at a wrong time, let him go to the village for alms at the right time; for ties ensnare the one that goes at a wrong time, therefore Buddhas do not go at a wrong time. (385)

12. 'Form, sound, taste, smell, and touch which intoxicate creatures, having subdued the desire for (all) these things (dhammas), let him in due time go in for his breakfast. (386)

13. 'And let the Bhikkhu, after having obtained his food at the right time and returned, sit down alone and privately; reflecting within himself let him not turn his mind to outward things, (but be) self-collected. (387)

14. 'If he speak with a Sâvaka or with anybody else, or with a Bhikkhu, let him talk about the excellent Dhamma, (but let him) not (utter) slander, nor blaming words against others. (388)

15. 'For some utter language contradicting others[1]; those narrow-minded ones we do not praise. Ties

[1. Vâdam hi eke patiseniyanti = virugghanti yugghitukâmâ hutvâ senâya patimukham gakkhantâ viya honti. Commentator.]

p. 65

from here and there ensnare them, and they send their mind far away in that (dispute). (389)

16. 'Let a Sâvaka of him with the excellent understanding (Buddha), after hearing the Dhamma taught by Sugata, discriminately seek for food, a monastery, a bed and a chair, and water for taking away the dirt of his clothes. (390)

17. 'But without clinging to these things, to food, to bed and chair, to water for taking away the dirt of his clothes, let a Bhikkhu be like a waterdrop on a lotus. (391)

18. 'A householder's work I will also tell you, how a Sâvaka is to act to be a good one; for that complete Bhikkhu-dhamma cannot be carried out by one who is taken up by (worldly) occupations. (392)

19. 'Let him not kill, nor cause to be killed any living being, nor

111

let him approve of others killing, after having refrained from hurting all creatures, both those that are strong and those that tremble in the world. (393)

20. 'Then let the Sâvaka abstain from (taking) anything in any place that has not been given (to him), knowing (it to belong to another), let him not cause any one to take, nor approve of those that take, let him avoid all (sort of) theft. (394)

21. ' Let the wise man avoid an unchaste life as a burning heap of coals; not being able to live a life of chastity, let him not transgress with another man's wife. (395)

22. 'Let no one speak falsely to another in the hall of justice or in the hall of the assembly, let him not cause (any one) to speak (falsely), nor approve of those that speak (falsely), let him avoid all (sort of) untruth. (396)

p. 66

23. 'Let the householder who approves of this Dhamma, not give himself to intoxicating drinks; let him not cause others to drink, nor approve of those that drink, knowing it to end in madness. (397)

24. 'For through intoxication the stupid commit sins and make

other people intoxicated; let him avoid this seat of sin, this madness, this folly, delightful to the stupid. (398)

25. 'Let him not kill any living being, let him not take what has not been given (to him), let him not speak falsely, and let him not drink intoxicating drinks, let him refrain from unchaste sexual intercourse, and let him not at night eat untimely food. (399)

26. 'Let him not wear wreaths nor use perfumes, let him lie on a couch spread on the earth:--this they call the eightfold abstinence (uposatha), proclaimed by Buddha, who has overcome pain. (400)

27. 'Then having with a believing mind kept abstinence (uposatha) on the fourteenth, fifteenth, and the eighth days of the half-month, and (having kept) the complete Pâtihârakapakkha[1] consisting of eight parts, (401)

28. 'And then in the morning, after having kept abstinence, let a wise man with a believing mind, gladdening the assembly of Bhikkhus with food and drink, make distributions according to his ability. (402)

29. 'Let him dutifully maintain his parents, and practise an honourable trade; the householder who observes this

strenuously goes to the gods by name, Sayampabhas.' (403)

Dhammikasutta is ended.

Kûlavagga is ended.

[1. Compare T. W. Rhys Davids, Buddhism, p. 141.]

III. MAHÂVAGGA.

1. PABBAGGÂSUTTA.

King Bimbisâra feeling interested in Buddha tries to tempt him with wealth, but is mildly rebuked by Buddha.

1. I will praise an ascetic life such as the clearly-seeing (Buddha) led, such as he thinking (over it) approved of as an ascetic life. (404)

2. ' This house-life is pain, the seat of impurity,' and 'an ascetic life is an open-air life,' so considering he embraced an ascetic life. (405)

3. Leading an ascetic life, he avoided with his body sinful deeds, and having (also) abandoned sin in words, he cleansed his life. (406)

4. Buddha went to Râgagaha, he entered the Giribbaga in Magadha for alms with a profusion of excellent signs. (407)

5. Bimbisâra standing in his palace saw him, and seeing him endowed with these signs, he spoke these words: (408)

6. 'Attend ye to this man, he is handsome, great, clean, he is both endowed with good conduct, and he does not look before him further than a yuga (the distance of a plough). (409)

7. 'With downcast eyes, thoughtful, this one is not like those of low caste; let the king's messengers run off, (and ask): "Where is the Bhikkhu going?"' (410)

8. The king's messengers followed after (him, and

p. 68

said): 'Where is the Bhikkhu going, where will he reside? (411)

9. 'Going begging from house to house, watching the door (of the senses), well restrained, he quickly filled his bowl, conscious, thoughtful. (412)

10. 'Wandering about in search of alms, having gone out of town, the Muni repaired to (the mountain) Pandava; it must be there he lives.' (413)

11. Seeing that he had entered his dwelling, the messengers then sat down, and one messenger having returned announced it to the king. (414)

12. 'This Bhikkhu, O great king, is sitting on the east side of Pandava, like a tiger, like a bull, like a lion in a mountain cave.' (415)

13. Having heard the messenger's words, the Khattiya in a fine chariot hastening went out to the Pandava mountain. (416)

14. Having gone as far as the ground was practicable for a chariot, the Khattiya, after alighting from the chariot, and approaching on foot, having come up (to him), seated himself. (417)

15. Having sat down the king then exchanged the usual ceremonious greetings with him, and after the complimentary talk he spoke these words: (418)

16. 'Thou art both young and delicate, a lad in his first youth, possessed of a fine complexion, like a high-born Khattiya. (419)

17. 'I will ornament the army-house, and at the head of the assembly of chiefs (nâga) give (thee) wealth; enjoy it and tell me thy birth, when asked.' (420)

18. Buddha: 'Just beside Himavanta, O king, there lives a people endowed with the power of wealth, the inhabitants of Kosala. (421)

p. 69

19. 'They are Âdikkas by family, Sâkiyas by birth; from that family I have wandered out, not longing for sensual pleasures. (422)

20. 'Seeing misery in sensual pleasures, and considering the forsaking of the world as happiness, I will go and exert myself; in this my mind delights.' (423)

Pabbaggâsutta is ended.

2. PADHÂNASUTTA.

Mâra tries to tempt Buddha, but disappointed is obliged to withdraw. Comp. Gospel of S. Matthew iv.

1. To me, whose mind was intent upon exertion near the river

Nerañgarâ, having exerted myself, and given myself to meditation for the sake of acquiring Nibbâna (yogakkhema), (424)

2. Came Namuki speaking words full of compassion: 'Thou art lean, ill-favoured, death is in thy neighbourhood. (425)

3. 'A thousandth part of thee (is the property) of death, (only) one part (belongs to) life; living life, O thou venerable one, is better; living thou wilt be able to do good works[1]. (426)

4. 'When thou livest a religious life, and feedest the sacrificial fire, manifold good works are woven to thee; what dost thou want with exertion? (427)

5. 'Difficult is the way of exertion, difficult to pass, difficult to enter upon;' saying these verses Mâra stood near Buddha. (428)

[1. Sahassabhâgo maranassa,
Ekamso tava gîvitam,
Gîvam bho gîvitam seyyo,
Gîvam puññâni kâhasi.]

p. 70

6. To Mâra thus speaking Bhagavat said this: 'O thou friend of the indolent, thou wicked one, for what purpose hast thou come here? (429)

7. 'Even the least good work is of no use to me; and what good works are required, Mâra ought to tell. (430)

8. 'I have faith and power, and understanding is found in me; while thus exerting myself, why do you ask me to live[1]? (431)

9. 'This (burning) wind will dry up even the currents of the rivers; should it not by degrees dry up my blood, while I am exerting myself? (432)

10. 'While the blood is drying up, the bile and the phlegm are dried up; while the flesh is wasting away, the mind gets more tranquil, and my attention, understanding, and meditation get more steadfast[2]. (433)

11. 'While I am living thus, after having felt the extreme sensations, my mind does not look for sensual pleasures; behold a being's purity. (434)

12. 'Lust thy first army is called, discontent thy second, thy third is called hunger and thirst, thy fourth desire. (435)

13. 'Thy fifth is called sloth and drowsiness, thy sixth cowardice, thy seventh doubt, thy eighth hypocrisy and stupor, (436)

14. 'Gain, fame, honour, and what celebrity has

[1. Evam mam pahitattam pi
Kim gîvam anupukkhasi.

2. Lohite sussamânamhi
Pittam semhañ ka sussati,
Mamsesu khîyamânesu
Bhiyyo kittam pasîdati
Bhiyyo sati ka paññâ ka
Samâdhi mama titthati.]

p. 71

been falsely obtained; and he who exalts himself and despises others[1]. (437)

15. 'This, O Namuki, is thine, the black one's, fighting army; none but a hero conquers it, and after conquering it obtains joy. (438)

16. 'Woe upon life in this world! death in battle is better for me than that I should live defeated. (439)

17. 'Plunged into this world some Samanas and Brâmanas are not seen, and they do not know the way in which the virtuous walk. (440)

18. 'Seeing on all sides an army arrayed, and Mâra on his elephant, I am going out to do battle, that he may not drive me away from my place. (441)

19. 'This army of thine, which the world of men and gods cannot conquer, I will crush with understanding as (one crushes) an unbaked earthen pot with a stone[2]. (442)

20. 'Having made my thought subject to me and my attention firm, I shall wander about from kingdom to kingdom, training disciples extensively. (443)

21. 'They (will be) zealous and energetic, executing my orders, (the orders) of one free from lust, and they will go (to the place) where, having gone, they will not mourn.' (444)

22. Mâra: 'For seven years I followed Bhagavat step by step; I

found no fault in the perfectly enlightened, thoughtful (Buddha). (445)

[1. Yo k' attânam samukkamse
Pare ka avagânati.

2. Yam te tam na-ppasahati
Senam loko sadevako
Tam te paññâya gakkhâmi[*]
Âmam pattam va amhanâ.

*. Instead of gakkhâmi I read bhañgâmi. Ba has vekkhâpi, Bi vegghâmi.]

p. 72

23. 'The crow hovered round the rock that looked like (a lump of) fat: "Do we here find something soft, is it something sweet?" (446)

24. 'Having obtained nothing sweet there, the crow went away from that spot. Thus like the crow approaching the rock, being disgusted, we shall go away from Gotama[1].' (447)

25. While overcome with sorrow the string of his lute slipped down; then that evil-minded Yakkha disappeared there. (448)

Padhânasutta is ended.

3. SUBHÂSITASUTTA.

On well-spoken language.
So it was heard by me:

At one time Bhagavat dwelt at Sâvatthî in Getavana. Bhagavat said this: 'O Bhikkhus, the speech that is provided with four requisites is well-spoken, not ill-spoken, both faultless and blameless to the wise.'

'Which four?'

'O Bhikkhus, the Bhikkhu speaks well-spoken (language), not ill-spoken; he speaks what is right (dhamma), not what is unrighteous (adhamma); he speaks what is pleasing, not what is unpleasing; he speaks what is true, not what is false. O Bhikkhus, the speech that is provided with these four requisites, is well-spoken, not ill-spoken, both faultless

[1. Kâko va selam âsagga[*].

Nibbiggâpema Gotamam[+].

+. Instead of Gotamam I read Gotamâ.]

p. 73

and blameless to the wise.' This said Bhagavat. When Sugata had said this, then the Master spoke the following:

1. 'Well-spoken language the just call the principal (thing); let one speak what is right (dhamma), not what is unrighteous (adhamma), that is the second; let one speak what is pleasing, not what is unpleasing, that is the third; let one speak what is true, not what is false, that is the fourth.' (449)

Then the venerable Vangîsa, rising from his seat, throwing his robe over one shoulder and bending his joined hands towards Bhagavat, said this: 'It occurs to me, O Sugata!'

'Let it occur to thee, O Vangîsa!' said Bhagavat.

Then the venerable Vangîsa, standing before Bhagavat, praised him with appropriate stanzas:

2. 'Let one say such words by which he does not pain himself, nor hurt others; such words are truly well-spoken. (450)

3. 'Let one speak pleasing words which are received joyfully (by all), and which (saying) he, without committing sins, speaks what is pleasing to others. (451)

4. 'Truth verily is immortal speech, this is a true saying; in what is true, in what is good, and in what is right, the just stand firm, so they say. (452)

5. 'The words which Buddha speaks, which are sure to bring about extinction and put an end to pain, such (words) are truly the best.' (453)

Subhâsitasutta is ended.

p. 74

4. SUNDARIKABHÂRADVÂGASUTTA.

Buddha shows to Sundarikabhâradvâga on whom to bestow oblations, and the Brâmana is finally converted.

So it was heard by me:

At one time Bhagavat dwelt in Kosala on the bank of the river Sundarikâ. And during that time the Brâmana Sundarikabhâradvâga made offerings to the fire and worshipped the fire. Then the Brâmana Sundarikabhâradvâga, having made offerings to the fire and worshipped the fire, and having risen from his seat, looked about him on all sides towards the four quarters of the globe, saying: 'Who is to enjoy the rest of this oblation?' The Brâmana Sundarikabhâradvâga saw Bhagavat sitting not far off at the root of a tree, wrapped up head and body; and seeing him he, after taking the rest of the oblation with his left hand and the waterpot with his right hand, went up to Bhagavat. Then Bhagavat, on hearing the footsteps of Sundarikabhâradvâga, the Brâmana, uncovered his head. Then the Brâhmana Sundarikabhâradvâga thought: 'This man is shaved, this man is a shaveling,' and he wished to return again from there. Then this came to the mind of Sundarikabhâradvâga, the Brâmana: 'Some Brâmanas also here are shaved, I think I shall go up and ask him about his descent.' Then the Brâhmana Sundarikabhâradvâga went up to Bhagavat, and having gone up he said this: 'Of what family art thou?'

Then Bhagavat answered Sundarikabhâradvâga, the Brâmana, in stanzas:

1. 'No Brâmana am I, nor a king's son, nor any

p. 75

Vessa; having thoroughly observed the class of common people, I wander about the world reflectingly, possessing nothing. (454)

2. 'Dressed in a sanghâti[1] and houseless I wander about, with my hair cut off, calm, not intermixing with people in this world. Thou askest me an unseasonable question about (my) family, O Brâhmana!' (455)

3. Sundarikabhâradvâga: 'Sir, Brâmanas together with Brâmanas ask truly, Art thou a Brâhmana?'

Bhagavat: 'If thou sayest, I am a Brâmana, and callest me no Brâmana, then I ask thee about the Sâvitti that consists of three padas and twenty-four syllables[2].' (456)

4. Sundarikabhâradvâga: 'For what (reason) did the Isis, men, Khattiyas, Brâmanas make offerings to the gods abundantly in this world?'

Bhagavat: 'He who, perfect and accomplished at the time of offering, obtains the ear of one or the other (god), he will succeed, so I say.' (457)

5. 'Surely his offering will bear fruit,'--so said the Brâmana,--'because we saw such an accomplished man; for by not seeing such as you, somebody else will enjoy the oblation.' (458)

6. Bhagavat: 'Therefore, O Brâmana, as you have come here to ask for something, ask; perhaps thou mightest here find one that is calm, without anger, free from pain, free from desire, one with a good understanding.' (459)

[1. See Rhys Davids, Buddhism, p. 166.

2. Tam Sâvittim pukkhâmi
Tipadam katuvîsatakkharam.
(Rig-veda III, 62, 10.)]

p. 76

7. Sundarikabhâradvâga: 'I delight in offering, O Gotama, I desire to make an offering, but I do not understand it; do thou instruct me, tell me in what case the offering succeeds.' (460)

8. Bhagavat: 'Therefore, O Brâmana, lend me thy ear, I will teach thee the Dhamma. (461)

9. 'Do not ask about descent, but ask about conduct; from wood, it is true, fire is born; (likewise) a firm Muni, although belonging to a low family, may become noble, when restrained (from sinning) by humility. (462)

10. 'He who is subdued by truth, endowed with temperance, accomplished, leading a religious life, on such a one in due time people should bestow oblations; let the Brâmana who has good works in view, offer. (463)

11. 'Those who, after leaving sensual pleasures, wander about houseless, well restrained, being like a straight shuttle, on such in due time people should bestow oblations; let the Brâmana who has good works in view, offer. (464)

12. 'Those whose passions are gone, whose senses are well composed, who are liberated like the moon out of the grasp of Râhu, on such in due time people should bestow oblations; let the Brâmana who has good works in view, offer. (465)

13. 'Those who wander about in the world without clinging (to anything), always thoughtful, having left selfishness, on such in due time people should bestow oblations; let the Brâmana who

has good works in view, offer. (466)

14. 'He who, after leaving sensual pleasures, wanders about victorious, he who knows the end of birth and death, who is perfectly happy (parinibbuta),

p. 77

calm like a deep water, Tathâgata deserves the oblation. (467)

15. 'Just with the just and far from the unjust[1], Tathâgata is possessed of infinite understanding; undefiled both in this world and in the other, Tathâgata deserves the oblation. (468)

16. 'He in whom there lives no deceit, no arrogance, he who is free from cupidity, free from selfishness, free from desire, who has banished anger, who is calm, the Brâmana who has removed the taint of grief, Tathâgata deserves the oblation. (469)

17. 'He who has banished (every) resting-place of the mind, he for whom there is no grasping, he who covets nothing either in this world or in the other, Tathâgata deserves the oblation[2]. (470)

18. 'He who is composed, who has crossed over the stream (of existence) and knows the Dhamma by (taking) the highest view (of it), he whose passions are destroyed, who is wearing the last body, Tathâgata deserves the oblation. (471)

19. 'He whose passion for existence and whose harsh talk are destroyed, are perished, (and therefore) exist not, he the accomplished and in every respect liberated Tathâgata deserves the oblation. (472)

20. 'He who has shaken off all ties, for whom there are no ties, who amongst arrogant beings is free from arrogance, having penetrated pain together with its domain and subject, Tathâgata deserves the oblation. (473)

21. 'He who, without giving himself up to desire, sees seclusion (i.e. Nibbâna), who has overcome the view that is to be taught by others, to whom there

[1. Samo samehi visamehi dûre.

2. Comp. Dhp. v. 20.]

p. 78

are no objects of sense whatever, Tathâgata deserves the oblation[1]. (474)

22. 'He to whom all Dhammas of every description, after he has penetrated them, are destroyed, are perished, (and therefore) exist not, he who is calm, liberated in the destruction of attachment (i.e. Nibbâna), Tathâgata deserves the oblation. (475)

23. 'He who sees the destruction of bond and birth, who has totally evaded the path of passion, (who is) pure, faultless, spotless, undepraved, Tathâgata deserves the oblation. (476)

24. 'He who does not measure himself by himself, who is composed, upright, firm, without desire, free from harshness (akhila), free from doubt, Tathâgata deserves the oblation. (477)

25. 'He to whom there is no cause of folly, who has a supernatural insight in all Dhammas, who wears the last body, and who has acquired perfect enlightenment, the highest, the blessed, (for him) thus a Yakkha's purification (takes place)[2].' (478)

26. Sundarikabhâradvâga: 'May my offering be a true offering, because I met with such a one out of the accomplished; Brahman is my witness, may Bhagavat accept me, may

Bhagavat enjoy my oblation.' (479)

27. Bhagavat: 'What is obtained by stanzas is not to be enjoyed by me, this is not the custom of the clearly-seeing, O Brâmana; Buddhas reject what is obtained by stanzas. While the Dhamma

[1. Âsam anissâya vivekadassî
Paravediyam[*] ditthim upâtivatto
Ârammanâ yassa na santi keki, &c.

2. Comp. Kalahavivâdasutta, v. 14.

*. Paravediyan ti parehi ñâpetabbam. Commentator.]

p. 79

exists, O Brâmana, this is the practice (of the Buddhas). (480)

28. 'With other food and drink must thou serve one that is perfect, a great Isi, whose passions are destroyed, and whose misbehaviour has ceased, for this is a field for one who looks for good works[1].' (481)

29. Sundarikabhâradvâga: 'Good, O Bhagavat, then I should like

to know, who will enjoy a gift from one like me, and whom I shall seek at the time of sacrifice (as one worthy of offerings) after having accepted thy doctrine.' (482)

30. Bhagavat: 'Whosoever has no quarrels, whose mind is untroubled, and who has freed himself from lusts, whose sloth is driven away, (483)

31. 'Whosoever conquers his sins, knows birth and death, the Muni who is endowed with wisdom[2], such a one who has resorted to offering, (484)

32. 'Him you should worship and honour with food and drink; so the gifts will prosper.' (485)

33. Sundarikabhâradvâga: 'Thou Buddha deservest the oblation, (thou art) the best field for good works, the object of offering to all the world; what is given to thee will bear great fruit.' (486)

Then the Brâmana Sundarikabhâradvâga said this to Bhagavat: 'It is excellent, O venerable Gotama! It is excellent, O venerable Gotama! As one raises what has been overthrown, or reveals what has been hidden, or tells the way to him who has gone astray, or holds out an oil lamp in the dark that those who have eyes may see the objects, even so by the venerable Gotama in manifold ways the Dhamma has been illustrated; I take refuge in

[1. Comp. Kasibhâradvâgsutta, v. 7.

2. Moneyyasampannam = paññâsampannam. Commentator.]

p. 80

the venerable Gotama, in the Dhamma, and in the Assembly of Bhikkhus; I wish to receive the robe and the orders from the venerable Gotama.'

The Brâmana Sundarikabhâradvâga received the pabbaggâ from Bhagavat, and he received also the upasampadâ; and the venerable Bhâradvâga, having lately received the upasampadâ, leading a solitary, retired, strenuous, ardent, energetic life, lived after having in a short time in this existence by his own understanding ascertained and possessed himself of that highest perfection of a religious life for the sake of which men of good family rightly wander away from their houses to a houseless state. 'Birth had been destroyed, a religious life had been led, what was to be done had been done, there was nothing else (to be done) for this existence,' so he perceived, and the venerable Bhâradvâga became one of the arahats.

Sundarikabhâradvâgasutta is ended.

5. MÂGHASUTTA.

Buddha on being asked tells Mâgha of those worthy of offerings and the blessing of offering.
So it was heard by me:

At one time Bhagavat dwelt at Râgagaha, in the mountain (called) the Vulture's Peak (Gigghakûta).

Then the young man Mâgha went to Bhagavat, and having gone to him he talked pleasantly with him, and after having had some pleasant, remarkable conversation with him he sat down apart; sitting down apart the young man Mâgha spoke this to Bhagavat:

p. 81

'O venerable Gotama, I am a liberal giver, bountiful, suitable to beg of; justly I seek for riches, and having sought for riches justly, I give out of the justly obtained and justly acquired riches to one, to two, to three, to four, to five, to six, to seven, to eight, to nine, to ten, to twenty, to thirty, to forty, to fifty, to a hundred, I give still more. (I should like to know), O venerable Gotama, whether I, while so giving, so offering, produce much good.'

'Certainly, O young man, dost thou in so offering produce much good; he, O young man, who is a liberal giver, bountiful, suitable to beg of, and who justly seeks for riches, and having sought for riches justly, gives out of his justly obtained and justly acquired riches to one, to two, to three, to four, to five, to six, to seven, to eight, to nine, to ten, to twenty, to thirty, to forty, to fifty, to a hundred, and gives still more, produces much good.'

Then the young man Mâgha addressed Bhagavat in stanzas:

1. 'I ask the venerable Gotama, the bountiful,'--so said the young man Mâgha,--'wearing the yellow robe, wandering about houseless:' 'He who is a householder, suitable to beg of, a donor, who, desirous of good, offers having what is good in view, and giving to others in this world food and drink,--where (i.e. on whom bestowed) will the oblation of such an offerer prosper?' (487)

2. 'He who is a householder, suitable to beg of, a donor, O Mâgha,'--so said Bhagavat,--'who, desirous of good, offers having what is good in view, and giving to others in this world food and drink, such a one will prosper with those worthy of offerings.' (488)

3. 'He who is a householder, suitable to beg of, a donor,'--so said the young man,--'who, desirous of good, offers having what is good in view, and giving to others in this world food and drink,--tell me (I being such a one), O Bhagavat, of those worthy of offerings.' (489)

4. Bhagavat: 'Those indeed who wander about in the world without clinging to anything and without possessing anything, perfect, self-restrained, on such in due time people should bestow oblations; let the Brâhmana who has good (works) in view, offer. (490)

5. 'Those who have cut through all bonds and fetters, who are subdued, liberated, free from pain, and free from desire, on such in due time people should bestow oblations; let the Brâmana who has good (works) in view, offer. (491)

6. 'Those who are released from all bonds, who are subdued, liberated, free from pain, and free from desire on such in due time people should bestow oblations; let the Brâmana who has good (works) in view, offer. (492)

7. 'Those who, having forsaken both passion and hatred and folly, have destroyed their desires and lead a religious life, on

such in due time people should bestow oblations; let the Brâhmana who has good (works) in view, offer[1]. (493)

8. 'Those in whom there lives no deceit, no arrogance, who are free from cupidity, free from selfishness, free from desire, on such in due time people should bestew oblations; let the Brâmana who has good (works) in view, offer. (494)

9. 'Those indeed who without being lost in desire,

[1. Comp. Dhp. v. 20.]

p. 83

after crossing the stream (of existence), wander about free from selfishness, on such in due time people should bestow oblations; let the Brâmana who has good (works) in view, offer. (495)

10. 'Those in whom there is no desire for anything in the world, nor for existence after existence here or in the other world, on such in due time people should bestow oblations; let the Brâmana who has good (works) in view, offer. (496)

11. 'Those who, after leaving sensual pleasures, wander about

houseless, well restrained, being like a straight shuttle, on such in due time people should bestow oblations; let the Brâmana who has good (works) in view, offer. (497)

12. 'Those whose passions are gone, whose senses are well composed, who are liberated like the moon out of the grasp of Râhu, on such in due time people should bestow oblations; let the Brâhmana who has good (works) in view, offer. (498)

13. 'Those who are calm, whose passions are gone, who are without anger, and for whom there is no transmigration after having left here, on such in due time people should bestow oblations; let the Brâhmana who has good (works) in view, offer. (499)

14. 'Those who, after leaving birth and death altogether, have conquered all doubt, on such in due time people should bestow oblations; let the Brâmana who has good (works) in view, offer. (500)

15. 'Those who wander about in the world with themselves for a light, not possessed of anything, in every respect liberated, on such in due time people should bestow oblations; let the Brâmana who has good (works) in view, offer. (501)

16. 'Those who in this world rightly understand

this: "This is the last (birth), there is no re-birth," on such in due time people should bestow oblations; let the Brâmana who has good (works) in view, offer. (502)

17. 'He who is accomplished, and delights in meditation, thoughtful, possessed of thorough enlightenment, a refuge for many, on such a one in due time people should bestow oblations; let the Brâhmana who has good (works) in view, offer.' (503)

18. 'Certainly my question was not in vain, Bhagavat has told me of those worthy of offerings; for thou truly knowest this in this world, as surely to thee this Dhamma is known. (504)

19. 'He who is a householder, suitable to beg of, a donor,'--so said the young man Mâgha,--'who, desirous of good, offers having what is good in view, and giving to others in this world food and drink,--tell me (I being such a one), O Bhagavat, of the blessing of offering.' (505)

20. 'Offer, O Mâgha,'--so said Bhagavat,--'and while offering make calm thy mind in all things; the object of the one that offers is the oblation, standing fast in this he leaves hatred

behind. (506)

21. 'Such a one whose passion is gone will repress hatred, cultivating an unbounded friendly mind; continually strenuous night and day he will spread infinite goodness through all regions.' (507)

22. Mâgha: 'Who prospers? who is liberated and who is bound? In which way can one by himself go to Brahmaloka? Tell this to me who does not know, O Muni, when asked. Bhagavat is indeed my witness that Brahman is seen by me to-day, for thou art to us equal to Brahman, this is the truth; how can one attain Brahmaloka, O thou glorious one?' (508)

p. 85

23. 'He who offers the threefold blessing of oblation, O Mâgha,'--so said Bhagavat,--'such a one will prosper with those worthy of offerings; so, having offered properly, he who is suitable to beg of attains Brahmaloka, so I say.' (509)

This having been said, Mâgha the young man spoke as follows to Bhagavat: 'Excellent, O venerable Gotama! Excellent, O venerable Gotama! As one raises what has been overthrown, or reveals what has been hidden, or tells the way to him who has gone astray, or holds out an oil lamp in the dark that those who have eyes may see the objects, even so by the venerable Gotama in manifold ways the Dhamma has been illustrated; I take refuge in the venerable Gotama and in the Dhamma and in the Assembly of Bhikkhus. Let the venerable Gotama accept me as an upâsaka (a follower, me), who henceforth for all my life have taken refuge (in him).'

Mâghasutta is ended.

6. SABHIYASUTTA.

Sabhiya, the Paribbâgaka, goes to the six famous teachers of his time to have his questions answered, but not having his doubts solved, he repairs to Gotama and asks him how one is to behave to become a Brâmana, a Samana, a Nahâtaka, a Khettagina, a Kusala, a Pandita, a Muni, a Vedagû, an Anuvidita, a Dhîra, an Âgâniya, a Sottiya, an Ariya, a Karanavat, a Paribbâgaka. Bhagavat answers his questions, and Sabhiya finally receives the robe and the orders from Buddha.
So it was heard by me:

At one time Bhagavat dwelt at Râgagaha, in Veluvana, in Kalandakanivâpa. And at that time questions were recited to Sabhiya, the Paribbâgaka

p. 86

(wandering mendicant), by an old benevolent deity: 'He who, O Sabhiya, be it a Samana or a Brâmana, explains these questions to thee when asked, near him thou shouldst live a religious life.'

Then Sabhiya, the Paribbâgaka, having learnt the questions from that deity, went to whatever Samanas and Brâmanas there were that had an assembly (of Bhikkhus), a crowd (of followers), and were well-known teachers, famous leaders, considered excellent by the multitude, as Pûrana-Kassapa, Makkhali-Gosâla, Agita-Kesakambali, Pakudha-Kakkâyana, Sañgaya-Belatthiputta, and Nigantha-Nâtaputta. Those he went to, and after going to them, he asked the questions. They, being asked the questions by Sabhiya, the Paribbâgaka, did not succeed (in answering them), and not succeeding, they showed wrath and hatred and discontent, and they also in return put questions to Sabhiya, the Paribbâgaka.

Then this came to the mind of Sabhiya, the Paribbâgaka: 'Whatever Samanas and Brâmanas there are that have an assembly (of Bhikkhus), a crowd (of followers), and are well-known teachers, famous leaders, considered excellent by the multitude, as Pûrana-Kassapa, Makkhali-Gosâla, Agita-Kesakambali, Pakudha-Kakkâyana, Sañgaya-Belatthiputta, and Nigantha-Nâtaputta, they, being asked questions by me, did not succeed (in answering them), and not succeeding they showed wrath and hatred and discontent, and they also in return put questions to me in this matter; surely I think I shall go back to what I have left, and enjoy sensual pleasures.

Then this came to the mind of Sabhiya, the Paribbâgaka: 'This Samana Gotama has both an

p. 87

assembly (of Bhikkhus) and a crowd (of followers), and is a well-known teacher, a famous leader, considered excellent by the multitude, surely I think I shall go to Samana Gotama and ask these questions.' Then this came to the mind of Sabhiya, the Paribbâgaka: 'Whatever Samanas and Brâhmanas there are that are decayed, old, aged, advanced in years, having reached old age, experienced elders, long ordained, having assemblies (of Bhikkhus), crowds (of followers), being teachers well-known, famous leaders, considered excellent by the multitude, as Pûrana-Kassapa, Makkhali-Gosâla, Agita-Kesakambali, Pakudha-Kakkâyana, Sañgaya-Belatthiputta, and Nigantha-Nâtaputta, they, being asked questions by me, did not succeed (in answering them), and not succeeding they showed wrath and hatred and discontent, and they also in return put questions to me in this matter; (I should like to know) whether Samana Gotama being asked these questions will be able to explain them to me, for Samana Gotama is both young by birth and new in ascetic life.'

Then this came to the mind of Sabhiya, the Paribbâgaka: 'Samana Gotama is not to be slighted because he is young; even if the Samana is young, yet he is mighty and powerful; surely I

146

think I shall go to Samana Gotama and ask these questions.' Then Sabhiya, the Paribbâgaka, went on a journey to Râgagaha, and wandering on his journey in regular order he came to Râgagaha, Veluvana, Kalandakanivâpa, to Bhagavat, and having come to Bhagavat he talked pleasantly with him, and after having had some pleasant and remarkable conversation with him he sat down apart; sitting down apart

p. 88

Sabhiya, the Paribbâgaka, spoke to Bhagavat in stanzas:

1. 'Anxious and doubtful I have come,'--so said Sabhiya,-- 'longing to ask questions. Do thou put an end to these (doubts when) asked these questions by me, in regular order, and rightly explain them to me.' (510)

2. 'Thou hast come from afar, O Sabhiya,'--so said Bhagavat,-- 'longing to ask questions; I shall put an end to those (doubts when) asked those questions by thee, in regular order, and rightly I shall explain them to thee. (511)

3. 'Ask me, O Sabhiya, a question; whatsoever thou wishest in thy mind that question I (will explain, and) put an end to (thy doubt).' (512)

Then this came to the mind of Sabhiya, the Paribbâgaka: 'It is marvellous, it is wonderful indeed, the reception which I did not get from other Samanas and Brâhmanas has been given me by Gotama,' so saying he glad, rejoicing, delighted, and highly elated asked Bhagavat a question:

4. 'What should a man (necessarily) have obtained that people may call him a Bhikkhu?'--so said Sabhiya,--'how may they call him compassionate, and how subdued? how can he be called enlightened (buddha)? Asked (about this) do thou, Bhagavat, explain it to me.' (513)

5. 'He who by the path he has himself made, O Sabhiya,'--so said Bhagavat,--'has attained to perfect happiness, who has conquered doubt, who lives after having left behind both gain and goods, who has destroyed re-birth, he is a Bhikkhu. (514)

6. 'Always resigned and attentive, he will not hurt any one in all the world, the Samana who has

p. 89

crossed the stream (of existence, and is) untroubled; for whom there are no desires (ussada), he is compassionate. (515)

148

7. 'He whose senses are trained internally and externally in all the world, he who after penetrating this and the other world longs for death, being trained, he is subdued. (516)

8. 'Whosoever, after having considered all times (kappa), the revolution (samsâra), both the vanishing and re-appearance (of beings), is free from defilement, free from sin, is pure, and has obtained destruction of birth, him they call enlightened (buddha).' (517)

Then Sabhiya, the Paribbâgaka, having approved of and rejoiced at the words of Bhagavat, glad, rejoicing, delighted, highly elated, asked Bhagavat another question:

9. 'What should a man (necessarily) have obtained that people may call him a Brâmana?'--so said Sabhiya,--'and how (may they call him) a Samana? and how a Nahâtaka? how can he be called a Nâga? Asked (about this) do thou Bhagavat explain it to me.' (518)

10. 'He who, after removing all sins, O Sabhiya,'--so said Bhagavat,--'is immaculate, well composed, firm-minded, perfect after crossing the Samsâra, such an independent one is called a Brâmana. (519)

11. 'He who is calm, having left behind good and evil, free from

defilement, having understood this and the other world, and conquered birth and death, such a one is called a Samana by being so[1].' (520)

12. 'Whosoever, after having washed away all sins internally and externally in all the world, does

[1. Samano tâdi pavukkate tathattâ.]

p. 90

not enter time (kappa) amongst gods and men who are subject to time, him they call a Nahâtaka (cleansed)[1]. (521)

13. 'He who does not commit any crime in the world, who, after abandoning all bonds and fetters, clings to nothing, being liberated, such a one is called a Nâga (sinless) by being so[2].' (522)

Then Sabhiya, the Paribbâgaka, having approved of and rejoiced at the words of Bhagavat, glad, rejoicing, delighted, highly elated, further asked Bhagavat a question:

14. 'Whom do the Buddhas call a Khettagina?'--so said Sabhiya,--'how (can they call any one) a Kusala? and how a Pandita? how

can he be called a Muni? Asked (about this) do thou Bhagavat explain it to me.' (523)

15. 'He who, after examining all regions, O Sabhiya,'--so said Bhagavat,--'the divine and the human, and Brahman's region, is delivered from the radical bond of all regions, such a one is called a Khettagina (he who has conquered the regions) by being so. (524)

16. 'He who, after examining all treasures, the divine and the human, and Brahman's treasure, is delivered from the radical bond of all treasures, such a one is called a Kusala (happy) by being so. (525)

17. 'He who, after examining both kinds of senses, internally and externally, is endowed with a

[1. Devamanussesu kappiyesu
Kappan n' eti tam âhu nahâtako.

2. Âgum na karoti kiñki loke
Sabbasamyoge visagga bandhanâni
Sabbattha na saggatî vimutto
Nâgo tâdi pavukkate tathattâ.
But compare Pabbaggâsutta 17, Mâgandiyasutta 11, &c.]

clear understanding and has conquered evil and good (kanhasukka), such a one is called a Pandita (wise) by being so. (526)

18. 'He who, having understood the Dhamma of the just and the unjust, internally and externally, in all the world, is to be worshipped by gods and men, he, after breaking through the net of ties, is called a Muni (sage).' (527)

Then Sabhiya, the Paribbâgaka, having approved of and rejoiced at the words of Bhagavat, glad, rejoicing, delighted, highly elated, further asked Bhagavat a question:

19. 'What should one (necessarily) have obtained that people may call him Vedagû?'--so said Sabhiya,--'and how (may they call him) Anuvidita? and how Viriyavat? How does one become Âgâniya? Asked (about this) do thou, O Bhagavat, explain it to me.' (528)

20. 'He who, having conquered all sensations, O Sabhiya,'--so said Bhagavat,--'which are (known) to Samanas and to Brâmanas, is free from passion for all sensations, he is Vedagû (having passed sensation) after conquering all sensation. (529)

21. 'He who, having seen the delusion of name and form[1], internally and externally, the root of sickness, and is delivered from the radical bond of all sickness, such a one is called Anuvidita (well-informed) by being so. (530)

22. 'He who is disgusted in this world with all sins, is strong after conquering the pain of hell, is strong and powerful, such a one is called Dhîra (= viriyavat, firm) by being so. (531)

[1. Anuvikka papaṅkanâmarûpam.]

p. 92

23. 'He whose bonds are cut off internally and externally, the root of ties[1], who is delivered from the radical bond of all ties, such a one is called Âgâniya (high-bred) by being so.' (532)

Then Sabhiya, the Paribbâgaka, having approved of and rejoiced at the words of Bhagavat, glad, rejoicing, delighted, highly elated, further asked Bhagavat a question:

24. 'What should a man (necessarily) have obtained that people may call him a Sottiya?'--so said Sabhiya,--'how (may they call him) an Ariya? and how a Karanavat? how may he become a

153

Paribbâgaka? Asked (about this) do thou, O Bhagavat, explain it to me.' (533)

25. 'Whosoever, after having heard and understood every Dhamma in the world, O Sabhiya,'--so said Bhagavat,-- 'whatsoever is wrong and whatsoever is blameless, is victorious, free from doubt, liberated, free from pain in every respect, him they call a Sottiya (learned in the revelation). (534)

26. 'Whosoever, after having cut off passions and desires, is wise and does not (again) enter the womb, having driven away the threefold sign, the mud (of lust), and who does not (again) enter time (kappa), him they call an Ariya (noble). (535)

27. 'He who in this world, after having attained the (highest) gain in the Karanas, is skilful, has always understood the Dhamma, clings to nothing, is liberated, and for whom there are no passions, he is a Karanavat (endowed with the obsrvances). (536)

28. 'Whosoever abstains from the action that has a painful result, above and below and across and in

[1. Yass' assu lutâni bandhanâni
Agghattam bahiddhâ ka sangamûlam.]

the middle, who wanders with understanding, who has put an end to deceit, arrogance, cupidity and anger, name and form, him they call a Paribbâgaka (a wandering mendicant) who has attained the (highest) gain.' (537)

Then Sabhiya, the Paribbâgaka, having approved of and rejoiced at the words of Bhagavat, glad, rejoicing, delighted, highly elated, having risen from his seat, and having put his upper robe upon one shoulder, bending his joined hands towards Bhagavat, praised Bhagavat face to face in appropriate stanzas:

29. 'Having conquered the three and sixty (philosophical) views referring to the disputations of the Samanas, thou hast crossed over the darkness of the stream[1]. (?) (538)

30. 'Thou hast passed to the end of and beyond pain, thou art a saint, perfectly enlightened, I consider thee one that has destroyed his passions, thou art glorious, thoughtful, of great understanding, O thou who puts an end to pain, thou hast carried me across. (539)

31. 'Because thou sawest my longing, and carriedst me across my doubt, adoration be to thee, O Muni, who hast attained the

(highest) gain in the ways of wisdom; O thou who art a true kinsman of the Âdikkas, thou art compassionate. (540)

32. 'The doubt I had before thou hast cleared away for me, O thou clearly-seeing; surely thou art a Muni, perfectly enlightened, there is no obstacle for thee. (541)

[1. Yâni ka tîni yâni ka satthi
Samanappavâdasitâni bhûripañña
Saññakkhara saññanissitâni (?)
Osaranâni vineyya oghatam' agâ.]

p. 94

33. 'And all thy troubles are scattered and cut off, thou art calm, subdued, firm, truthful. (542)

34. 'All gods and both Nârada and Pabbata rejoice at thee, the chief of the sinless (nâganâga), the great hero, when thou art speaking. (543)

35. 'Adoration be to thee, O noble man, adoration be to thee, O thou best of men; in the world of men and gods there is no man equal to thee. (544)

156

36. 'Thou art Buddha, thou art the Master, thou art the Muni that conquers Mâra; after having cut off desire thou hast crossed over and hast carried across this generation. (545)

37. 'The elements of existence (upadhi) are overcome by thee, the passions are destroyed by thee, thou art a lion, free from desire, thou hast left behind fear and terror. (546)

38. 'As a beautiful lotus does not adhere to the water, so thou dost not cling to good and evil, to either; stretch forth thy feet, O hero, Sabbiya worships the Master's (feet).' (547)

Then Sabhiya, the Paribbâgaka, stooping with his head to Bhagavat's feet, said this to Bhagavat:

'It is excellent, O venerable! It is excellent, O venerable! As one raises what has been overthrown, or reveals what has been hidden, or tells the way to him who has gone astray, or holds out an oil lamp in the dark that those who have eyes may see the objects, even so by the venerable Gotama in manifold ways the Dhamma has been illustrated; I take refuge in the venerable Gotama, in the Dhamma, and in the Assembly of Bhikkhus; I wish to receive the robe and the orders from the venerable Bhagavat.'

'He who, O Sabhiya, formerly belonging

another creed (aññatitthiyapubba), wishes to be adopted into this religion (dhammavinaya), and wishes to receive the robe and the orders, he serves for four months; after the lapse of four months Bhikkhus who have appeased their thoughts will give him the robe and the orders to become a Bhikkhu, (for) I also in this matter acknowledge difference of persons.'

'If, O venerable, those that formerly belonged to another creed and wish to be adopted into this religion and to receive the robe and the orders, serve for four months, and after the lapse of four months Bhikkhus who have appeased their thoughts give them the robe and the orders that they may become Bhikkhus, I will (also) serve for four months, and after the lapse of four months Bhikkhus who have appeased their thoughts shall give (me) the robe and the orders that I may become a Bhikkhu.'

Sabhiya, the Paribbâgaka, received the robe and the orders from Bhagavat, and the venerable Sabhiya, having lately received the upasampadâ, leading a solitary, retired, strenuous, ardent, energetic life, lived after having in a short time in this existence by his own understanding ascertained and possessed himself of that highest perfection of a religious life for the sake of which men of good family rightly wander away from their houses to a houseless state. 'Birth had been destroyed, a religious life had been led, what was to be done had been done, there was nothing else (to be done) for this existence,' so he perceived, and the venerable Sabhiya became one of the saints.

Sabhiyasutta is ended.

p. 96

7. SELASUTTA.

Keniya, the Gatila, invites Buddha with his assembly to take his meals with him on the morrow. Sela, the Brâmana, arrived at that place with his three hundred young men; seeing the preparations he asks what is going on, and is answered that Buddha is expected the next day. On hearing the word 'Buddha,' Sela asks where Buddha lives, goes to him, converses with him, and is converted; so are his followers.
So it was heard by me:

At one time Bhagavat wandering about in Anguttarâpa, with a large assembly of Bhikkhus, with 1250 Bhikkhus, went to Âpana, a town in Anguttarâpa.

And Keniya, the ascetic, with matted hair (gatila) heard the following: 'The Samana, the venerable Gotama, the Sakya son, gone out from the family of the Sakyas, wandering about in Anguttarâpa with a large assembly of Bhikkhus, with 1250 Bhikkhus, has reached Âpana, and the following good praising words met the venerable Gotama: "And so he is Bhagavat, the venerable, the perfectly enlightened, endowed with science and works (viggâkarana), the happy, knowing the world, the incomparable, the charioteer of men that are to be subdued, the master, the enlightened of gods and men, the glorious; he teaches this world and the world of gods, of Mâras, of Brahmans, and beings comprising Samanas and Brâmanas, gods and men, having himself known and seen them face to face; he teaches the Dhamma (which is) good in the beginning, in the middle, and in the end, is full of meaning and rich in words, quite complete; he teaches a religious life, and good is the sight of such saints.'"

Then Keniya, the Gatila, went (to the place) where

p. 97

Bhagavat was, and having gone there he talked pleasantly with him, and after having had some pleasant and remarkable conversation (with him) he sat down apart; and while Keniya, the Gatila, was sitting down apart, Bhagavat, by religious talk, taught, advised, roused, and delighted him. Then Keniya, the Gatila, having been taught, advised, roused, and delighted by Bhagavat through religious talk, said this to Bhagavat:

'Let the venerable Gotama accept my food tomorrow, together with the assembly of Bhikkhus.'

This having been said, Bhagavat answered Keniya, the Gatila: 'Large, O Keniya, is the assembly of Bhikkhus, one thousand two hundred and fifty Bhikkhus, and thou art intimate with the Brâmanas.'

A second time Keniya, the Gatila, said this to Bhagavat: 'Although, O venerable Gotama, the assembly of Bhikkhus is large, one thousand two hundred and fifty Bhikkhus, and I am intimate with the Brâmanas, let the venerable Gotama accept my food to-morrow, together with the assembly of Bhikkhus.'

A second time Bhagavat said this to Keniya, the Gatila: 'Large, O Keniya, is the assembly of Bhikkhus, one thousand two hundred and fifty Bhikkhus, and thou art intimate with the Brâmanas.'

A third time Keniya, the Gatila, said this to Bhagavat: 'Although, O venerable Gotama, the assembly of Bhikkhus is large, one thousand two hundred and fifty Bhikkhus, and I am intimate with the Brâhmanas, yet let the venerable Gotama accept my food to-morrow, together with the assembly of Bhikkhus.' Bhagavat assented by being silent.

Then Keniya, the Gatila, having learnt the assent of Bhagavat, after rising from his seat went to his hermitage, and having gone there he addressed his friends and servants, his relatives and kinsmen (as follows): 'Let my venerable friends and servants, relatives and kinsmen hear me;--the Samana Gotama has been invited by me to (take his) food (with me) to-morrow, together with the assembly of Bhikkhus; wherefore you must render me bodily service.'

'Surely, O venerable one,' so saying the friends and servants, relatives and kinsmen of Keniya, the Gatila, complying with his request, some of them dug fireplaces, some chopped firewood, some washed the vessels, some placed waterpots, some prepared seats. Keniya, the Gatila, on the other hand, himself provided a circular pavilion.

At that time the Brâmana Sela lived at Âpana, perfect in the three Vedas, vocabulary, Ketubha, etymology, Itihâsa as the fifth (Veda), versed in metre, a grammarian, one not deficient in popular controversy and the signs of a great man, he taught three hundred young men the hymns[1]. At that time Keniya, the Gatila, was intimate with the Brâhmana Sela. Then the Brâmana Sela surrounded by three hundred young men, walking on foot, arrived at the place where the hermitage of Keniya, the Gatila, was. And the Brâmana Sela saw the Gatilas in Keniya's hermitage, some of them digging fireplaces, some chopping firewood, some washing the vessels, some placing waterpots, some

[1. Tena kho pana samayena. Selo brâhmano Âpane pativasati tinnam vedânam pâragû sanighanduketubhânam sâkkharappabhedânam itihâsapañkamânam padako veyyâkarano lokâyatamahâpurisalakkhanesu anavayo tîni mânavakasatâni mante vâketi.]

p. 99

preparing seats, and Keniya, the Gatila, on the other hand, himself providing a circular pavilion; seeing Keniya, the Gatila, he said this: 'Is the venerable Keniya to celebrate the marriage of a son or the marriage of a daughter, or is there a great sacrifice at hand, or has Bimbisâra, the king of Magadha, who has a large body of troops, been invited for to-morrow, together with his army?'

'I am not to celebrate the marriage of a son or the marriage of a daughter, nor has Bimbisâra, the king of Magadha, who has a large body of troops, been invited for to-morrow, together with his army, yet a great sacrifice of mine is at hand. The Samana Gotama, the Sakya son, gone out from the Sakya family, wandering about in Anguttarâpa with a large assembly of Bhikkhus, one thousand two hundred and fifty Bhikkhus, has reached Âpana, and the following good praising words met the venerable Gotama: "And so he is Bhagavat, the venerable, the perfectly enlightened, endowed with science and works (viggâkarana), the happy, knowing the world, the incomparable, the charioteer of men that are to be subdued, the master, the enlightened of gods and men, the glorious, he has been invited by me for to-morrow, together with the assembly of Bhikkhus."'

'Didst thou say that he is a Buddha, O venerable Keniya?'

'Yes, I say, O venerable Sela, that he is a Buddha.'

'Didst thou say that he is a Buddha, O venerable Keniya? ,

'Yes, I say, O venerable Sela, that he is a Buddha.'

Then this occurred to the Brâhmana Sela: 'This sound "Buddha" is (indeed) rare, but in our hymns

p. 100

are to be found the thirty-two signs of a great man, and for a great man endowed with these there are two conditions, and no more: if he lives in a house he is a king, a universal (king), a just religious king, a lord of the four-cornered (earth), a conqueror, one who has obtained the security of his people (and) is possessed of the seven gems. These are his seven gems, namely, the wheel gem, the elephant gem, the horse gem, the pearl gem, the woman gem, the householder gem, and the chief gem as the seventh. He has more than a thousand sons, heroes, possessing great bodily strength and crushing foreign armies; he having conquered this ocean-girt earth without a rod and without a weapon, but by justice, lives (in a house). But if, on the other hand, he goes out from (his) house to the houseless state, he becomes a saint, a perfectly enlightened, one who has removed the veil in the world. And where, O venerable Keniya, dwells now that venerable Gotama, the saint and the perfectly enlightened?'

This having been said, Keniya, the Gatila, stretching out his right arm, spoke as follows to the Brâmana Sela: 'There, where yon blue forest line is, O venerable Sela.'

Then the Brâmana Sela together with (his) three hundred young men went to the place where Bhagavat was. Then the Brâmana Sela addressed those young men: 'Come ye, venerable ones, with but little noise, walking step by step, for Bhagavats are difficult of access, walking alone like lions, and when I speak to the venerable Samana Gotama, do ye not utter interrupting words, but wait ye venerable ones, for the end of my speech.'

Then the Brâmana Sela went to the place where

Bhagavat was, and having gone there he talked pleasantly with Bhagavat, and after having had some pleasant and remarkable conversation with him he sat down apart, and while sitting down apart Sela, the Brâhmana, looked for the thirty-two signs of a great man on the body of Bhagavat. And the Brâmana Sela saw the thirty-two signs of a great man on the body of Bhagavat with the exception of two; in respect to two of the signs of a great man he had doubts, he hesitated, he was not satisfied, he was not assured as to the member being enclosed in a membrane and as to his having a large tongue.

Then this occurred to Bhagavat: 'This Brâmana Sela sees in me the thirty-two signs of a great man with the exception of two, in respect to two of the signs of a great man he has doubts, he hesitates, he is not satisfied, he is not assured as to the member being enclosed in a membrane, and as to my having a large tongue.' Then Bhagavat created such a miraculous creature that the Brâmana Sela might see Bhagavat's member enclosed in a membrane. Then Bhagavat having put out his tongue touched and stroked both his ears, touched and stroked both nostrils, and the whole circumference of his forehead he covered with his tongue.

Then this occurred to the Brâhmana Sela: 'The Samana Gotama is endowed with the thirty-two signs of a great man, with them all, not with (only) some of them, and yet I do not know whether he is a Buddha or not; I have heard old and aged

Brâhmanas, teachers and their previous teachers, say that those who are saints and perfectly enlightened manifest themselves when their praise is uttered. I think I shall praise the Samana Gotama face to

p. 102

face in suitable stanzas.' Then the Brâmana Sela praised Bhagavat face to face in suitable stanzas:

1. 'Thou hast a perfect body, thou art resplendent, well-born, of beautiful aspect, thou hast a golden colour, O Bhagavat, thou hast very white teeth, thou art strong. (548)

2. 'All the signs that are for a well-born man, they are on thy body, the signs of a great man. (549)

3. 'Thou hast a bright eye, a handsome countenance, thou art great, straight, majestic, thou shinest like a sun in the midst of the assembly of the Samanas. (550)

4. 'Thou art a Bhikkhu of a lovely appearance, thou hast a skin like gold; what is the use of being a Samana to thee who art possessed of the highest beauty? (551)

5. 'Thou deservest to be a king, a king of universal kings, a ruler of the four-cornered (earth), a conqueror, a lord of the jambu grove (i.e. India). (552)

6. 'Khattiyas and wealthy kings are devoted to thee; rule, O Gotama, as a king of kings, a leader of men.' (553)

7. 'I am a king, O Sela,'--so said Bhagavat,--'an incomparable, religious king (dhammarâgan), with justice (dhammena) I turn the wheel, a wheel that is irresistible[1].' (554)

8. 'Thou acknowledgest thyself (to be) perfectly enlightened (sambuddha),'--so said Sela, the Brâhmana,--'an incomparable, religious king; "with justice I turn the wheel," so thou sayest, O Gotama. (555)

[1. Compare Gospel of S. John xviii. 37.]

p. 103

9. 'Who is thy general, (who is thy) disciple, (who is) the successor of the master, who is to turn after thee the wheel of religion turned (by thee)? ' (556)

10. 'The wheel turned by me, O Sela,'--so said Bhagavat,--'the incomparable wheel of religion, Sâriputta is to turn after (me), he taking after Tathâgata. (557)

11. 'What is to be known is known (by me), what is to be cultivated is cultivated (by me), what is to be left is left by me, therefore I am a Buddha, O Brâmana. (558)

12. 'Subdue thy doubt about me, have faith (in me), O Brâmana, difficult (to obtain) is the sight of Buddhas repeatedly. (559)

13. 'Of those whose manifestation is difficult for you (to obtain) in the world repeatedly, I am, O Brâmana, a perfectly enlightened, an incomparable physician, (560)

14. 'Most eminent, matchless, a crusher of Mâra's army; having subjected all enemies I rejoice secure on every side.' (561)

15. Sela: 'O venerable ones, pay attention to this: as the clearly-seeing (Buddha) says, (so it is): he is a physician, a great hero, and roars like a lion in the forest. (562)

16. 'Who, having seen him, the most eminent, the matchless, the crusher of Mâra's army, is not appeased, even if he be, of black origin (kanhâbhigâtika). (563)

17. 'He who likes me, let him follow after (me), he who does not like me, let him go away; I shall at once take the orders in the presence of him of excellent understanding (i.e. Buddha).' (564)

p. 104

18. The followers of Sela: 'If this doctrine of the perfectly enlightened pleases thee, we also shall take the orders in the presence of him of excellent understanding.' (565)

19. These three hundred Brâmanas asked with clasped hands (to be admitted into the order): 'We want to cultivate a religious life, O Bhagavat, in thy presence.' (566)

20. 'A religious life is well taught (by me), O Sela,'--so said Bhagavat,--'an instantaneous, an immediate (life), in which it is not in vain to become an ascetic to one who learns in earnest[1].' (567)

Then the Brâmana Sela together with his assembly took the robe and the orders in the presence of Bhagavat.

Then Keniya, the Gatila, by the expiration of that night, having provided in his hermitage nice hard food and soft food, let

Bhagavat know the time (of the meal): 'It is time, O venerable Gotama, the meal is prepared.' Then Bhagavat in the morning, having put on his raiment and taken his bowl and robes, went to the Gatila Keniya's hermitage, and having gone there he sat down on the prepared seat, together with the assembly of Bhikkhus. Then Keniya, the Gatila, satisfied and served with his own hands the assembly of Bhikkhus, with Buddha at their head, with nice hard food and soft food. Then Keniya, the Gatila, having gone up to Bhagavat who had finished eating and had taken his hand out of the bowl, took a low seat and sat down apart, and

[1. Svâkkhâtam brahmakariyam
Sanditthikam akâlikam
Yattha amoghâ pabbaggâ
Appamattassa sikkhato.]

p. 105

while Keniya, the Gatila, was sitting down apart, Bhagavat delighted him with these stanzas:

21. 'The principal thing in sacrifice is the sacred fire, the principal thing amongst the hymns is the Sâvitti[1], the king is the principal amongst men, and the sea the principal amongst waters (nadînam[2]). (568)

22. 'Amongst the stars the moon is the principal thing, the sun is the principal thing amongst the burning[3] (objects), amongst those that wish for good works and make offerings the assembly (samgha) indeed is the principal.' (569)

Then Bhagavat, having delighted Keniya, the Gatila, with these stanzas, rose from (his) seat and went away.

Then the venerable Sela together with his assembly leading a solitary, retired, strenuous, ardent, energetic life, lived after having in a short time in this existence by his own understanding ascertained and possessed himself of that highest perfection of a religious life for the sake of which men of good family rightly wander away from their houses to a houseless state; 'birth (had been) destroyed, a religious life (had been) led, what was to be done (had been) done, there was nothing else (to be done) for this existence,' so he perceived, and the venerable Sela together with his assembly became one of the saints.

Then the venerable Sela together with his assembly went to Bhagavat, and having gone (to him) he put his upper robe on one shoulder, and bending his joined hands towards Bhagavat he addressed him in stanzas:

[1. Sâvittî khandaso mukham.

172

2. Comp. Nâlakasutta v. 42.

3. Âdikko tapatam mukham.]

p. 106

23. 'Because we took refuge in thee on the eighth day previous to this, O thou clearly-seeing, in seven nights, O Bhagavat, we have been trained in thy doctrine. (570)

24. 'Thou art Buddha, thou art the Master, thou art the Muni that conquered Mâra, thou hast, after cutting off the affections, crossed over (the stream of existence) and taken over these beings. (571)

25. 'The elements of existence (upadhi) have been overcome by thee, the passions have been destroyed by thee, thou art a lion not seizing on anything, thou hast left behind fear and danger. (572)

26. 'These three hundred Bhikkhus stand here with clasped hands; stretch out thy feet, O hero, let the Nâgas worship the Master's feet.' (573)

Selasutta is ended.

8. SALLASUTTA.

Life is short, all mortals are subject to death, but knowing the terms of the world the wise do not grieve, and those who have left sorrow will be blessed.--Text in the Dasaratha-Gâtaka, p. 34. 1. Without a cause and unknown is the life of mortals in this world, troubled and brief, and combined with pain. (574)

2. For there is not any means by which those that have been born can avoid dying; after reaching old age there is death, of such a nature are living beings. (575)

3. As ripe fruits are early in danger of falling, so mortals when born are always in danger of death. (576)

4. As all earthen vessels made by the potter end in being broken, so is the life of mortals. (577)

p. 107

5. Both young and grown-up men, both those who are fools and those who are wise men, all fall into the power of death, all are

174

subject to death. (578)

6. Of those who, overcome by death, go to the other world, a father does not save his son, nor relatives their relations. (579)

7. Mark! while relatives are looking on and lamenting greatly, one by one of the mortals is carried off, like an ox that is going to be killed. (580)

8. So the world is afflicted with death and decay, therefore the wise do not grieve, knowing the terms of the world. (581)

9. For him, whose way thou dost not know, either when he is coming or when he is going, not seeing both ends, thou grievest in vain. (582)

10. If he who grieves gains anything, (although he is only) a fool hurting himself, let the wise man do the same. (583)

11. Not from weeping nor from grieving will any one obtain peace of mind; (on the contrary), the greater his pain will be, and his body will suffer. (584)

12. He will be lean and pale, hurting himself by himself, (and

yet) the dead are not saved, lamentation (therefore) is of no avail. (585)

13. He who does not leave grief behind, goes (only) deeper into pain; bewailing the dead he falls into the power of grief. (586)

14. Look at others passing away, men that go (to what they deserve) according to their deeds, beings trembling already here, after falling into the power of death. (587)

15. In whatever manner people think (it will come to pass), different from that it becomes, so great is

p. 108

the disappointment[1] (in this world); see, (such are) the terms of the world. (588)

16. Even if a man lives a hundred years or even more, he is at last separated from the company of his relatives, and leaves life in this world. (589)

17. Therefore let one, hearing (the words of) the saint, subdue his lamentation; seeing the one that has passed away and is dead, (let him say): 'He will not be found by me (any more).'

18. As a house on fire is extinguished by water, so also the wise, sensible, learned, clever man rapidly drives away sorrow that has arisen, as the wind a tuft of cotton. (591)

19. He who seeks his own happiness should draw out his arrow (which is) his lamentation, and complaint, and grief. (592)

20. He who has drawn out the arrow and is not dependent (on anything) will obtain peace of mind; he who has overcome all sorrow will become free from sorrow, and blessed (nibbuta). (593)

Sallasutta is ended.

9. VÂSETTHASUTTA.

A dispute arose between two young men, Bhâradvâga and Vâsettha, the former contending man to be a Brâmana by birth, the latter by deeds. They agreed to go and ask Samana Gotama, and he answered that man is a Brâmana by his work only. The two young men are converted.--Text (from Magghimanikâya) and translation in Alwis's Buddhist Nirvâna, p. 103.
So it was heard by me:

At one time Bhagavat dwelt at Ikkhânamkala, in the Ikkhânamkala forest. At that time many distinguished,

[1. Etâdiso vinâbhâvo.]

p. 109

wealthy Brâmanas lived at Ikkhânamkala, as the Brâmana Kamkin, the Brâmana Târukkha, the Brâmana Pokkharasâti, the Brâhmana Gânussoni, the Brâmana Todeyya, and other distinguished, wealthy Brâmanas.

Then this dialogue arose between the young men Vâsettha and Bhâradvâga while walking about:

'How does one become a Brâmana?'

The young man Bhâradvâga said: 'When one is noble by birth on both sides, on the mother's and on the father's side, of pure conception up to the seventh generation of ancestors, not discarded and not reproached in point of birth, in this way one is a Brâmana.'

The young man Vâsettha said: 'When one is virtuous and endowed with (holy) works, in this way he is a Brâmana.'

Neither could the young man Bhâradvâga convince the young man Vâsettha, nor could the young man Vâsettha convince the young man Bhâradvâga. Then the young man Vâsettha addressed the young man Bhâradvâga: 'O Bhâradvâga, this Samana Gotama, the Sakya son, gone out from the Sakya family, dwells at Ikkhânamkala, in the forest of Ikkhânamkala, and the following good praising words met the venerable Gotama: "And so he is Bhagavat, the venerable, the enlightened, the glorious, let us go, O venerable Bhâradvâga, let us go (to the place) where the Samana Gotama is, and having gone there let us ask the Samana Gotama about this matter, and as the Samana Gotama replies so will we understand it."'

'Very well, O venerable one;' so the young man Bhâradvâga answered the young man Vâsettha.

p. 110

Then the young men Vâsettha and Bhâradvâga went (to the place) where Bhagavat was, and having gone, they talked pleasantly with Bhagavat, and after having had some pleasant and remarkable conversation (with him) they sat down apart. Sitting down apart the young man Vâsettha addressed Bhagavat in stanzas:

1. 'We are accepted and acknowledged masters of the three Vedas[1], I am (a pupil) of Pokkharasâti, and this young man is (the pupil) of Târukkha. (594)

2. 'We are accomplished in all the knowledge propounded by those who are acquainted with the three Vedas, we are padakas (versed in the metre), veyyâkaranas (grammarians?), and equal to our teachers in recitation (gappa)[2]. (595)

3. 'We have a controversy regarding (the distinctions of) birth, O Gotama! Bhâradvâga says, one is a Brâmana by birth, and I say, by deeds; know this, O thou clearly-seeing! (596)

4. 'We are both unable to convince each other, (therefore) we have come to ask thee (who art) celebrated as perfectly enlightened. (597)

5. 'As people adoring the full moon worship (her) with uplifted clasped hands, so (they worship) Gotama in the world. (598)

6. 'We ask Gotama who has come as an eye to the world: Is a man a Brâhmana by birth, or is he so

[1. Anuññâtapatiññâtâ

180

Tevigga mayam asm' ubho.

2. Teviggânam[*] yad akkhâtam
Tatra kevalino 'smase,
Padak' asmâ veyyâkaranâ,
Gappe[+] âkariyasâdisâ.

*. Teviggânam = tivedânam. Commentator; but compare v. 63.

+. Gappe = vede. Commentator.]

p. 111

by deeds? Tell us who do not know, that we may know a Brâmana.' (599)

7. 'I will explain to you, O Vâsettha,'--so said Bhagavat,--'in due order the exact distinction of living beings according to species, for their species are manifold. (600)

8. 'Know ye the grass and the trees, although they do not exhibit (it), the marks that constitute species are for them, and (their) species are manifold. (601)

9. 'Then (know ye) the worms, and the moths, and the different sorts of ants, the marks that constitute species are for them, and (their) species are manifold. (602)

10. 'Know ye also the four-footed (animals), small and great, the marks that constitute species are for them, and (their) species are manifold. (603)

11. 'Know ye also the serpents, the long-backed snakes, the marks that constitute species are for them, and (their) species are manifold. (604)

12. 'Then know ye also the fish which range in the water, the marks that constitute species are for them, and (their) species are manifold. (605)

13. 'Then know ye also the birds that are borne along on wings and move through the air, the marks that constitute species are for them, and (their) species are manifold. (606)

14. 'As in these species the marks that constitute species are abundant, so in men the marks that constitute species are not abundant. (607)

15. 'Not as regards their hair, head, ears, eyes, mouth, nose, lips,

or brows, (608)

16. 'Nor as regards their neck, shoulders, belly, back, hip, breast, female organ, sexual intercourse, (609)

p. 112

17. 'Nor as regards their hands, feet, palms, nails, calves, thighs, colour, or voice are there marks that constitute species as in other species. (610)

18. 'Difference there is in beings endowed with bodies, but amongst men this is not the case, the difference amongst men is nominal (only)[1]. (611)

19. 'For whoever amongst men lives by cowkeeping,--know this, O Vâsettha,--he is a husbandman, not a Brâmana.' (612)

20. 'And whoever amongst men lives by different mechanical arts,--know this, O Vâsettha,--he is an artisan, not a Brâmana. (613)

21. 'And whoever amongst men lives by trade,--know this, O Vâsettha,--he is a merchant, not a Brâmana. (614)

22. And whoever amongst men lives by serving others,--know this, O Vâsettha,--he is a servant, not a Brâhmana. (615)

23. 'And whoever amongst men lives by theft,--know this, O Vâsettha,--he is a thief, not a Brâhmana. (616)

24. 'And whoever amongst men lives by archery,--know this, O Vâsettha,--he is a soldier, not a Brâmana. (617)

25. 'And whoever amongst men lives by performing household ceremonials,--know this, O Vâsettha,--he is a sacrificer, not a Brâmana. (618)

26. 'And whoever amongst men possesses villages and countries,--know this, O Vâsettha,--he is a king, not a Brâmana. (619)

[1. Pakkattam sasarîresu,
Manussesv-etam na viggati,
Vokâran ka manussesu
Samaññâya pavukkati.]

p. 113

27. 'And I do not call one a Brâmana on account of his birth or of his origin from (a particular) mother; he may be called bhovâdi, and he may be wealthy, (but) the one who is possessed of nothing and seizes upon nothing, him I call a Brâhmana[1]. (620)

28. 'Whosoever, after cutting all bonds, does not tremble, has shaken off (all) ties and is liberated, him I call a Brâmana. (621)

29. 'The man who, after cutting the strap (i.e. enmity), the thong (i.e. attachment), and the rope (i.e. scepticism) with all that pertains to it, has destroyed (all) obstacles (i.e. ignorance), the enlightened (buddha), him I call a Brâmana. (622)

30. 'Whosoever, being innocent, endures reproach, blows, and bonds, the man who is strong in (his) endurance and has for his army this strength, him I call a Brâmana. (623)

31. 'The man who is free from anger, endowed with (holy) works, virtuous, without desire, subdued, and wearing the last body, him I call a Brâhmana. (624)

32. 'The man who, like water on a lotus leaf, or a mustard seed on the point of a needle, does not cling to sensual pleasures, him I call a Brâhmana. (625)

33. 'The man who knows in this world the destruction of his pain, who has laid aside (his) burden, and is liberated, him I call a Brâmana. (626)

34. 'The man who has a profound understanding, who is wise, who knows the true way and the wrong way, who has attained the highest good, him I call a Brâmana. (627)

[1. Comp. Dhp. v. 396, &c.]

p. 114

35. 'The man who does not mix with householders nor with the houseless, who wanders about without a house, and who has few wants, him I call a Brâhmana. (628)

36. 'Whosoever, after refraining from hurting (living) creatures, (both) those that tremble and those that are strong, does not kill or cause to be killed, him I call a Brâmana. (629)

37. 'The man who is not hostile amongst the hostile, who is peaceful amongst the violent, not seizing (upon anything) amongst those that seize (upon everything), him I call a Brâmana. (630)

38. 'The man whose passion and hatred, arrogance and hypocrisy have dropt like a mustard seed from the point of a needle, him I call a Brâmana. (631)

39. 'The man that utters true speech, instructive and free from harshness, by which he does not offend any one, him I call a Brâmana. (632)

40. 'Whosoever in the world does not take what has not been given (to him), be it long or short, small or large, good or bad, him I call a Brâhmana. (633)

41. 'The man who has no desire for this world or the next, who is desireless and liberated, him I call a Brâmana. (634)

42. 'The man who has no desire, who knowingly is free from doubt; and has attained the depth of immortality, him I call a Brâmana. (635)

43. 'Whosoever in this world has overcome good and evil, both ties, who is free from grief and defilement, and is pure, him I call a Brâmana. (636)

44. 'The man that is stainless like the moon, pure, serene, and undisturbed, who has destroyed joy, him I call a Brâmana. (637)

p. 115

45. 'Whosoever has passed over this quagmire difficult to pass, (who has passed over) revolution (samsâra) and folly, who has crossed over, who has reached the other shore, who is meditative, free from desire and doubt, calm without seizing (upon anything), him I call a Brâmana. (638)

46. 'Whosoever in this world, after abandoning sensual pleasures, wanders about houseless, and has destroyed the existence of sensual pleasures (kâmabhava), him I call a Brâmana. (639)

47. 'Whosoever in this world, after abandoning desire, wanders about houseless, and has destroyed the existence of desire (tanhâbhava), him I call a Brâmana. (640)

48. 'Whosoever, after leaving human attachment (yoga), has overcome divine attachment, and is liberated from all attachment, him I call a Brâhmana. (641)

49. 'The man that, after leaving pleasure and disgust, is calm and free from the elements of existence (nirupadhi), who is a

188

hero, and has conquered all the world, him I call a Brâmana. (642)

50. 'Whosoever knows wholly the vanishing and reappearance of beings, does not cling to (anything); is happy (sugata), and enlightened, him I call a Brâmana. (643)

51. 'The man whose way neither gods nor Gandhabbas nbr men know, and whose passions are destroyed, who is a saint, him I call a Brâmana. (644)

52. 'The man for whom there is nothing, neither before nor after nor in the middle, who possesses nothing, and does not seize (upon anything), him I call a Brâmana. (645)

53. 'The (man that is undaunted like a) bull, who

p. 116

is eminent, a hero, a great sage (mahesi), victorious, free from desire, purified, enlightened, him I call a Brâmana. (646)

54. 'The man who knows his former dwellings, who sees both heaven and hell, and has reached the destruction of births, him

I call a Brâmana. (647)

55. 'For what has been designated as "name" and "family" in the world is only a term, what has been designated here and there is understood by common consent[1]. (648)

56. 'Adhered to for a long time are the views of the ignorant, the ignorant tell us, one is a Brâmana by birth. (649)

57. 'Not by birth is one a Brâmana, nor is one by birth no Brâmana; by work (kammanâ) one is a Brâmana, by work one is no Brâmana. (650)

58. 'By work one is a husbandman, by work one is an artisan, by work one is a merchant, by work one is a servant. (651)

59. 'By work one is a thief, by work one is a soldier, by work one is a sacrificer, by work one is a king. (652)

60. 'So the wise, who see the cause of things and understand the result of work, know this work as it really is[2]. (653)

61. 'By work the world exists, by work mankind

[1. Samaññâ h' esâ lokasmim
Nâmagottam pakappitam,
Sammukkâ samudâgatam
Tattha tattha pakappitam.

2. Evam etam yathâbhûtam
Kammam passanti panditâ
Patikkasamuppâdadasâ
Kammavipâkakovidâ.]

p. 117

exists, beings are bound by work as the linch-pin of the rolling cart (keeps the wheel on)[1]. (654)

62. 'By penance, by a religious life, by self-restraint, and by temperance, by this one is a Brâmana, such a one (they call) the best Brâmana. (655)

63. 'He who is endowed with the threefold knowledge[2], is calm, and has destroyed regeneration,--know this, O Vâsettha,-- he is to the wise Brahman and Sakka.' (656)

This having been said, the young men Vâsettha and Bhâradvâga spoke to Bhagavat as follows:

'It is excellent, O venerable Gotama! It is excellent, O venerable Gotama! As one raises what has been overthrown, or reveals what has been hidden, or tells the way to him who has gone astray, or holds out an oil lamp in the dark that those who have eyes may see the objects, even so by the venerable Gotama in manifold ways the Dhamma has been illustrated; we take refuge in the venerable Gotama, in the Dhamma, and in the Assembly of Bhikkhus; may the venerable Gotama receive us as followers (upâsaka), who from this day for life have taken refuge (in him).'

Vâsetthasutta is ended.

[1. Kammanâ vattatî loko,
Kammanâ vattatî pagâ,
Kammanibandhanâ sattâ
Rathasânîva yâyato.

2. Tîhi viggâhi sampanno.]

p. 118

10. KOKÂLIYASUTTA.

Kokâliya abuses Sâriputta and Moggallâna to Buddha; therefore as soon as he has left Buddha, he is struck with boils, dies and goes to the Paduma hell, whereupon Buddha describes to the Bhikkhus the punishment of backbiters in hell.
So it was heard by me:

At one time Bhagavat dwelt at Sâvatthî, in Getavana, in the park of Anâthapindika. Then the Bhikkhu Kokâliya approached Bhagavat, and after having approached and saluted Bhagavat he sat down apart; sitting down apart the Bhikkhu Kokâliya said this to Bhagavat: "O thou venerable one, Sâriputta and Moggallâna have evil desires, they have fallen into the power of evil desires.'

When this had been said, Bhagavat spoke to the Bhikkhu Kokâliya as follows: '(Do) not (say) so, Kokâliya; (do) not (say) so, Kokâliya; appease, O Kokâliya, (thy) mind in regard to Sâriputta and Moggallâna: Sâriputta and Moggallâna are amiable[1].'

A second time the Bhikkhu Kokâliya said this to Bhagavat: 'Although thou, O venerable Bhagavat, (appearest) to me (to be) faithful and trustworthy, yet Sâriputta and Moggallâna have evil desires, they have fallen into the power of evil desires.'

A second time Bhagavat said this to the Bhikkhu Kokâliya: '(Do) not (say) so, Kokâliya; (do) not (say) so, Kokâliya; appease, O Kokâliya, (thy) mind in regard to Sâriputta and Moggallâna:

Sâriputta and Moggallâna are amiable.'

A third time the Bhikkhu Kokâliya said this to Bhagavat: 'Although thou, O venerable Bhagavat, (appearest) to me (to be) faithful and trustworthy,

[1. Pesalâ ti piyasîlâ. Commentator.]

p. 119

yet Sâriputta and Moggallâna have evil desires, Sâriputta and Moggallâna have fallen into the power of evil desires.'

A third time Bhagavat said this to the Bhikkhu Kokâliya: '(Do) not (say) so, Kokâliya; (do) not (say) so, Kokâliya; appease, O Kokâliya, (thy) mind in regard to Sâriputta and Moggallâna: Sâriputta and Moggallâna are amiable.'

Then the Bhikkhu Kokâliya, after having risen from his seat and saluted Bhagavat and walked round him towards the right, went away; and when he had been gone a short time, all his body was struck with boils as large as mustard seeds; after being only as large as mustard seeds, they became as large as kidney beans; after being only as large as kidney beans, they became as large as chick peas; after being only as large as chick peas, they became as large as a Kolatthi egg (?); after being only as large as

194

a Kolatthi egg, they became as large as the jujube fruit; after being only as large as the jujube fruit, they became as large as the fruit of the emblic myrobalan; after being only as large as the fruit of the emblic myrobalan, they became as large as the unripe beluva fruit; after being only as large as the unripe beluva fruit, they became as large as a billi fruit (?); after being as large as a billi fruit, they broke, and matter and blood flowed out. Then the Bhikkhu Kokâliya died of that disease, and when he had died the Bhikkhu Kokâliya went to the Paduma hell, having shown a hostile mind against Sâriputta and Moggallâna. Then when the night had passed Brahman Sahampati of a beautiful appearance, having lit up all Getavana, approached Bhagavat, and having approached and saluted Bhagavat,

p. 120

he stood apart, and standing apart Brahman Sahampati said this to Bhagavat: 'O thou venerable one, Kokâliya, the Bhikkhu, is dead and after death, O thou venerable one, the Bhikkhu Kokâliya is gone to the Paduma hell, having shown a hostile mind against Sâriputta and Moggallâna.'

This said Brahman Sahampati, and after saying this and saluting Bhagavat, and walking round him towards the right, he disappeared there.

Then Bhagavat, after the expiration of that night, addressed the

Bhikkhus thus: 'Last night, O Bhikkhus, when the night had (nearly) passed, Brahman Sahampati of a beautiful appearance, having lit up all Getavana, approached Bhagavat, and having approached and saluted Bhagavat, he stood apart, and standing apart Brahman Sahampati said this to Bhagavat: "O thou venerable one, Kokâliya, the Bhikkhu, is dead; and after death, O thou venerable one, the Bhikkhu Kokâliya is gone to the Paduma hell, having shown a hostile mind against Sâriputta and Moggallâna." This said Brahman Sahampati, O Bhikkhus, and having said this and saluted me, and walked round me towards the right, he disappeared there.'

When this had been said, a Bhikkhu asked Bhagavat: 'How long is the rate of life, O venerable one, in the Paduma hell?'

'Long, O Bhikkhu, is the rate of life in the Paduma hell, it is not easy to calculate either (by saying) so many years or so many hundreds of years or so many thousands of years or so many hundred thousands of years.'

'But it is possible, I suppose, to make a comparison, O thou venerable one?'

p. 121

'It is possible, O Bhikkhu;' so saying, Bhagavat spoke (as follows): 'Even as, O Bhikkhu, (if there were) a Kosala load of

196

sesamum seed containing twenty khâris, and a man after the lapse of every hundred years were to take from it one sesamum seed at a time, then that Kosala load of sesamum seed, containing twenty khâris, would, O Bhikkhu, sooner by this means dwindle away and be used up than one Abbuda hell; and even as are twenty Abbuda hells, O Bhikkhu, so is one Nirabbuda hell; and even as are twenty Nirabbuda hells, O Bhikkhu, so is one Ababa hell; and even as are twenty Ababa hells, O Bhikkhu, so is one Ahaha hell; and even as are twenty Ahaha hells, O Bhikkhu, so is one Atata hell; and even as are twenty Atata hells, O Bhikkhu, so is one Kumuda hell; and even as are twenty Kumuda hells, O Bhikkhu, so is one Sogandhika hell; and even as are twenty Sogandhika hells, O Bhikkhu, so is one Uppalaka hell; and even as are twenty Uppalaka hells, O Bhikkhu, so is one Pundarîka hell; and even as are twenty Pundarîka hells, O Bhikkhu, so is one Paduma hell; and to the Paduma hell, O Bhikkhu, the Bhikkhu Kokâliya is gone, having shown a hostile mind against Sâriputta and Moggallâna.' This said Bhagavat, and having said this Sugata, the Master, furthermore spoke as follows:

1. 'To (every) man that is born, an axe is born in his mouth, by which the fool cuts himself, when speaking bad language. (657)

2. 'He who praises him who is to be blamed or blames him who as to be praised, gathers up sin in his mouth, and through that (sin) he will not find any joy. (658)

p. 122

3. 'Trifling is the sin that (consists in) losing riches by dice; this is a greater sin that corrupts the mind against Sugatas. (659)

4. 'Out of the one hundred thousand Nirabbudas (he goes) to thirty-six, and to five Abbudas; because he blames an Ariya he goes to hell, having employed his speech and mind badly. (660)

5. 'He who speaks falsely goes to hell, or he who having done something says, "I have not done it;" both these after death become equal, in another world (they are both) men guilty of a mean deed[1]. (661)

6. 'He who offends an offenceless man, a pure man, free from sin, such a fool the evil (deed) reverts against, like fine dust thrown against the wind[2]. (662)

7. 'He who is given to the quality of covetousness, such a one censures others in his speech, (being himself) unbelieving, stingy, wanting in affability, niggardly, given to backbiting. (663)

8. 'O thou foul-mouthed, false, ignoble, blasting, wicked, evil-doing, low, sinful, base-born man, do not be garrulous in this world, (else) thou wilt be an inhabitant of hell[3]. (664)

9. 'Thou spreadest pollution to the misfortune (of others), thou revilest the just, committing sin (yourself), and having done many evil deeds thou wilt go to the pool (of hell) for a long time. (665)

[1. Comp. Dhp. v. 306.

2. Comp. Dhp. v. 125.

3. Mukhadugga vibhûta-m-anariya
Bhûnahu[*] pâpaka dukkatakâri
Purisanta kalî avagâta
Mâ bahubhâni dha nerayiko si.

*. Bhûnahu bhûtihanaka vuddhinâsaka. Commentator.]

p. 123

110. 'For one's deeds are not lost, they will surely come (back to you), (their) master will meet with them, the fool who commits sin will feel the pain in himself in the other world[1]. (666)

11. 'To the place where one is struck with iron rods, to the iron stake with sharp edges he goes; then there is (for him) food as appropriate, resembling a red-hot ball of iron. (667)

12. 'For those who have anything to say (there) do not say fine things, they do not approach (with pleasing faces); they do not find refuge (from their sufferings), they lie on spread embers, they enter a blazing pyre. (668)

13. 'Covering (them) with a net they kill (them) there with iron hammers; they go to dense darkness[2], for that is spread out like the body of the earth. (669)

14. 'Then (they enter) an iron pot, they enter a blazing pyre, for they are boiled in those (iron pots) for a long time, jumping up and down in the pyre. (670)

15. 'Then he who commits sin is surely boiled in a mixture of matter and blood; whatever quarter he inhabits, he becomes rotten there from coming in contact (with matter and blood). (671)

16. 'He who commits sin will surely be boiled in the water, the dwelling-place of worms; there it is not (possible) to get to the shore, for the jars (are) exactly alike[3]. (?) (672)

[1. Comp. Revelation xiv. 13.

2. Andham va Timisam âyanti.

3. Pulavâvasathe salilasmim
Tattha kim pakkati kibbisakârî,
Gantum na hi tîram p' atthi
Sabbasamâ hi samantakapallâ.]

p. 124

17. 'Again they enter the sharp Asipattavana with mangled limbs; having seized the tongue with a hook, the different watchmen (of hell) kill (them). (673)

18. 'Then they enter Vetaranî, that is difficult to cross and has got streams of razors with sharp edges; there the fools fall in, the evil-doers after having done evil. (674)

19. 'There black, mottled flocks of ravens eat them who are weeping, and dogs, jackals, great vultures, falcons, crows tear (them). (675)

20. 'Miserable indeed is the life here (in hell) which the man

sees that commits sin. Therefore should a man in this world for the rest of his life be strenuous, and not indolent. (676)

21. 'Those loads of sesamum seed which are carried in Paduma hell have been counted by the wise, they are (several) nahutas and five kotis, and twelve hundred kotis besides[1]. (677)

22. 'As long as hells are called painful in this world, so long people will have to live there for a long time; therefore amongst those who have pure, amiable, and good qualities one should always guard speech and mind.' (678)

Kokâliyasutta is ended.

11. NÂLAKASUTTA.

The Isi Asita, also called Kanhasiri, on seeing the gods rejoicing, asks the cause of it, and having heard that Buddha has been born, he descends from Tusita heaven. When the Sakyas showed the child to him, he received it joyfully and prophesied
[1. Nahutâni hi kotiyo pañka bhavanti
Dvâdasa kotisatâni pun' aññâ.]
p. 125

about it. Buddha explains to Nâlaka, the sister's son of Asita, the highest state of wisdom.--Compare Lalita-vistara, Adhyâya VII;

202

Asita and Buddha, or the Indian Simeon, by J. Muir, in the Indian Antiquary, Sept. 1878.
Vatthugâthâ.

1. The Isi Asita saw in (their) resting-places during the day the joyful, delighted flocks of the Tidasa gods, and the gods in bright clothes, always highly praising Inda, after taking their clothes and waving them. (679)

2. Seeing the gods with pleased minds, delighted, and showing his respect, he said this on that occasion: 'Why is the assembly of the gods so exceedingly pleased, why do they take their clothes and wave them? (680)

3. 'When there was an encounter with the Asuras, a victory for the gods, and the Asuras were defeated, then there was not such a rejoicing. What wonderful (thing) have the gods seen that they are so delighted? (681)

4. 'They shout and sing and make music, they throw (about their) arms and dance; I ask you, the inhabitants of the tops of (mount) Meru, remove my doubt quickly, O venerable ones!' (682)

5. 'The Bodhisatta, the excellent pearl, the incomparable, is born for the good and for a blessing in the world of men, in the

town of the Sakyas, in the country of Lumbinî. Therefore we are glad and exceedingly pleased. (683)

6. 'He, the most excellent of all beings, the preeminent man, the bull of men, the most excellent of all creatures will turn the wheel (of the Dhamma) in the forest called after the Isis, (he who is) like the roaring lion, the strong lord of beasts.' (684)

p. 126

7. Having heard that noise he descended from (the heaven of) Tusita. Then he went to Suddhodana's palace, and having sat down there he said this to the Sakyas: 'Where is the prince? I wish to see (him).' (685)

8. Then the Sakyas showed to (the Isi), called Asita, the child, the prince who was like shining gold, manufactured by a very skilful (smith) in the mouth of a forge, and beaming in glory and having a beautiful appearance. (686)

9. Seeing the prince shining like fire, bright like the bull of stars wandering in the sky, like the burning sun in autumn, free from clouds, he joyfully obtained great delight. (687)

10. The gods held in the sky a parasol with a thousand circles and numerous branches, yaks' tails with golden sticks were

fanned, but those who held the yaks' tails and the parasol were not seen. (688)

11. The Isi with the matted hair, by name Kanhasiri, on seeing the yellow blankets (shining) like a golden coin, and the white parasol held over his head, received him delighted and happy. (689)

12. And having received the bull of the Sakyas, he who was wishing to receive him and knew the signs and the hymns, with pleased thoughts raised his voice, saying: 'Without superior is this, the most excellent of men.' (690)

13. Then remembering his own migration he was displeased and shed tears; seeing this the Sakyas asked the weeping Isi, whether there would be any obstacle in the prince's path. (691)

14. Seeing the Sakyas displeased the Isi said: 'I do not remember anything (that will be) unlucky for the prince, there will be no obstacles at

p. 127

all for him, for this is no inferior (person). Be without anxiety. (692)

15. ' This prince will reach the summit of perfect enlightenment, he will turn the wheel of the Dhamma, he who sees what is exceedingly pure (i.e. Nibbâna), this (prince) feels for the welfare of the multitude, and his religion[1] will be widely spread. (693)

16. 'My life here will shortly be at an end, in the middle (of his life) there will be death for me; I shall not hear the Dhamma of the incomparable one; therefore I am afflicted, unfortunate, and suffering.' (694)

17. Having afforded the Sakyas great joy he went out from the interior of the town to lead a religious life; but taking pity on his sister's son, he induced him to embrace the Dhamma of the incomparable one. (695)

18. 'When thou hearest from others the sound "Buddha," (or) "he who has acquired perfect enlightenment walks the way of the Dhamma," then going there and enquiring about the particulars, lead a religious life with that Bhagavat.' (696)

19. Instructed by him, the friendly-minded, by one who saw in the future what is exceedingly pure (i.e. Nibbâna), he, Nâlaka, with a heap of gathered-up good works, and with guarded senses dwelt (with him), looking forward to Gina (i.e. Buddha). (697)

20. Hearing the noise, while the excellent Gina turned the wheel (of the Dhamma), and going and seeing the bull of the Isis, he, after being converted,

[1. Brahmakariyam = sâsanam. Commentator.]

p. 128

asked the eminent Muni about the best wisdom, when the time of Asita's order had come. (698)

The Vatthugâthâs are ended.

21. 'These words of Asita are acknowledged true (by me), therefore we ask thee, O Gotama, who art perfect in all things (dhamma). (699)

22. 'O Muni, to me who am houseless, and who wish to embrace a Bhikkhu's life, explain when asked the highest state, the state of wisdom (moneyya).' (700)

23. 'I will declare to thee the state of wisdom,'--so said

Bhagavat,--'difficult to carry out, and difficult to obtain; come, I will explain it to thee, stand fast, be firm. (701)

24. 'Let a man cultivate equanimity: which is (both) reviled and praised in the village, let him take care not to corrupt his mind, let him live calm, and without pride. (702)

25. 'Various (objects) disappear, like a flame of fire in the wood[1]; women tempt the Muni, let them not tempt him. (703)

26. 'Let him be disgusted with sexual intercourse, having left behind sensual pleasures of all kinds, being inoffensive and dispassionate towards living creatures, towards anything that is feeble or strong. (704)

27. 'As I am so are these, as these are so am I, identifying himself with others, let him not kill nor cause (any one) to kill[2]. (705)

[1. Ukkâvakâ nikkharanti
Dâye aggisikhûpamâ.

2. Yathâ aham tathâ ete
Yathâ ete tathâ aham
Attânam upamam katvâ
Na haneyya na ghâtaye.

p. 129

28. 'Having abdoned desire and covetousness let him act as one that sees clearly where a common man sticks, let him cross over this hell. (706)

29. 'Let him be with an empty stomach, taking little food, let him have few wants and not be covetous; not being consumed by desire he will without desire be happy. (707)

30. 'Let the Muni, after going about for alms, repair to the outskirts of the wood, let him go and sit down near the root of a tree. (708)

31. 'Applying himself to meditation, and being wise, let him find his pleasure in the outskirts of the wood, let him meditate at the root of a tree enjoying himself. (709)

32. 'Then when night is passing away let him repair to the outskirts of the village, let him not delight in being invited nor in what is brought away from the village. (710)

33. 'Let not the Muni, after going to the village, walk about to the houses in haste; cutting off (all) talk while seeking food, let him not utter any coherent speech[1]. (711)

34. '"What I have obtained that is good," "I did not get (anything that is) good," so thinking in both cases he returns to the tree unchanged[2]. (712)

35. "Wandering about with his alms-bowl in his

[1. Na vâkam payutam bhane.

2. Alattham yad idam sâdhu
Nâlattham kusalam iti,
Ubhayen' eva so tâdi[*]
Rukkham va upanivattati.

*. Tâdi = nibbikâro. Commentator.]

p. 130

hand, considered dumb without being dumb, let him not blush at a little gift, let him not despise the giver. (713)

210

36. 'Various are the practices illustrated by the Samana, they do not go twice to the other shore, this (is) not once thought[1]. (?) (714)

37. 'For whom there is no desire, for the Bhikkhu who has cut off the stream (of existence) and abandoned all kinds of work, there is no pain. (715)

38. 'I will declare to thee the state of wisdom,'--so said Bhagavat,--'let one be like the edge of a razor, having struck his palate with his tongue, let him be restrained in (regard to his) stomach. (716)

39. 'Let his mind be free from attachment, let him not think much[2] (about worldly affairs), let him be without defilement, independent, and devoted to a religious life. (717)

40. 'For the sake of a solitary life and for the sake of the service that is to be carried out by Samanas, let him learn, solitariness is called wisdom[3]; alone indeed he will find pleasure. (718)

41. 'Then he will shine through the ten regions, having heard the voice of the wise, of the meditating, of those that have abandoned sensual pleasures, let my adherent then still more devote himself to modesty and belief. (719)

42. 'Understand this from the waters in chasms

[1. Ukkâvakâ hi patipadâ
Samanena pakâsitâ,
Na pâram digunam yanti,
Na idam ekagunam mutam.

2. Na kâpi bahu kintaye.

3. Ekattam monam akkhâtam.]

p. 131

and cracks: noisy go the small waters, silent goes the vast ocean[1]. (720)

43. 'What is deficient that makes a noise, what is full that is calm; the fool is like a half-(filled) water-pot, the wise is like a full pool. (721)

44. 'When the Samana speaks much that is possessed of good sense, he teaches the Dhamma while knowing it, while knowing it he speaks much[2]. (722)

45. 'But he who while knowing it is self-restrained, and while knowing it does not speak much, such a Muni deserves wisdom (mona), such a Muni has attained to wisdom (mona)[3].' (723)

Nâlakasutta is ended.

12. DVAYATÂNUPASSANÂSUTTA.

All pain in the world arises from upadhi, aviggâ, samkhârâ viññâna, phassa, vedanâ, tanhâ, upâdâna, ârambha, âhâra, iñgita, nissaya, rûpa, mosadhamma, sukha.
So it was heard by me:

At one time Bhagavat dwelt at Sâvatthî in Pubbârâma, Migâramâtar's mansion. At that time Bhagavat on the Uposatha day[4], on the fifteenth,

[1. Tan nadîhi vigânâtha
Sobbhesu padaresu ka:
Sanantâ yanti kussobbhâ
Tunhî yâti mahodadhi.

2. Yam samano bahu bhâsati
Upetam atthasamhitam

213

Gânam so dhammam deseti
Gânam so bahu bhâsati.

3. Yo ka gânam samyatatto
Gânam na bahu bhâsati
Sa munî monam arahati
Sa munî monam agghagâ.

4. See Rhys Davids, Buddhism, p. 140.]

p. 132

it being full moon, in the evening was sitting in the open air, surrounded by the assembly of Bhikkhus. Then Bhagavat surveying the silent assembly of Bhikkhus addressed them (as follows):

'Whichever Dhammas there are, O Bhikkhus, good, noble, liberating, leading to perfect enlightenment,--what is the use to you of listening to these good, noble, liberating Dhammas, leading to perfect enlightenment? If, O Bhikkhus, there should be people that ask so, they shall be answered thus: "Yes, for the right understanding of the two Dhammas." "Which two do you mean?" "(I mean), this is pain, this is the origin of pain," this is one consideration, "this is the destruction of pain, this is the way leading to the destruction of pain," this is the second consideration; thus, O Bhikkhus, by the Bhikkhu that considers

214

the Dyad duly[1], is strenuous, ardent, resolute, of two fruits one fruit is to be expected: in this world perfect knowledge, or, if any of the (five) attributes still remain, the state of an Anâgâmin (one that does not return).' This said Bhagavat, (and) when Sugata had said this, the Master further spoke:

1. 'Those who do not understand pain and the origin of pain, and where pain wholly and totally is stopped, and do not know the way that leads to the cessation of pain, (724)

2. 'They, deprived of the emancipation of thought

[1. . . . . kâ upanisâ savanâyâ,'ti iti ke bhikknave pukkhitâro assu te evam assu vakanîyâ: yâvad eva dvayatânam dhammânam yathâbhûtam ñânâyâ 'ti, kiñka dvayatam vadetha? 'idam dukkham, ayam dukkhasamudayo' ti ayam ekânupassanâ, 'ayam dukkhanirodho, ayam dukkhanirodhagâminî patipadâ' ti ayam dutiyânupassanâ; evam sammâdvayatânupassino . . .]

p. 133

and the emancipation of knowledge, are unable to put an end (to samsâra), they will verily continue to undergo birth and decay. (725)

3. 'And those who understand pain and the origin of pain, and where pain wholly and totally is stopped, and who know the way that leads to the cessation of pain, (726)

4. 'They, endowed with the emancipation of thought and the emancipation of knowledge, are able to put an end (to samsâra), they will not undergo birth and decay. (727)

'"Should there be a perfect consideration of the Dyad in another way," if, O Bhikkhus, there are people that ask so, they shall be told, there is, and how there is: "Whatever pain arises is all in consequence of the upadhis (elements of existence)," this is one consideration, "but from the complete destruction of the upadhis, through absence of passion, there is no origin of pain," this is the second consideration; thus, O Bhikkhus, by the Bhikkhu that considers the Dyad duly, that is strenuous, ardent, resolute, of two fruits one fruit is to be expected: in this world perfect knowledge, or, if any of the (five) attributes still remain, the state of an Anâgâmin (one that does not return).' This said Bhagavat, (and) when Sugata had said this, the Master further spoke:

5. 'Whatever pains there are in the world, of many kinds, they arise having their cause in the upadhis; he who being ignorant creates upadhi, that fool again undergoes pain; therefore being wise do not create upadhi, considering what is the birth and origin of pain. (728)

'"Should there be a perfect consideration of the

p. 134

Dyad in another way," if, O Bhikkhus, there are people that ask so, they shall be told, there is, and how there is: "Whatever pain arises is all in consequence of avigga (ignorance)," this is one consideration, "but from the complete destruction of avigga, through absence of passion, there is no origin of pain," this is the second consideration; thus, O Bhikkhus, by the Bhikkhu that considers the Dyad duly, that is strenuous, ardent, resolute, of two fruits one fruit is to be expected: in this world perfect knowledge, or, if any of the (five) attributes still remain, the state of an Anâgâmin (one that does not return).' This said Bhagavat, (and) when Sugata had said this, the Master further spoke:

6. 'Those who again and again go to samsâra with birth and death, to existence in this way or in that way,--that is the state of avigga. (729)

7. 'For this avigga is the great folly by which this (existence) has been traversed long, but those beings who resort to knowledge do not go to rebirth. (730)

'"Should there be a perfect consideration of the Dyad in

another way," if, O Bhikkhus, there are people that ask so, they shall be told, there is, and how there is: "Whatever pain arises is all in consequence of the samkhâras (matter)," this is one consideration, "but from the complete destruction of the samkhâras, through absence of passion, there is no origin of pain," this is the second consideration; thus, O Bhikkhus, by the Bhikkhu that considers the Dyad duly, that is strenuous, ardent, resolute, of two fruits one fruit is to be expected: in this world perfect knowledge, or, if any of the (five) attributes still remain, the state

p. 135

of an Anâgâmin (one that does not return).' This said Bhagavat; (and) when Sugata had said this, the Master further spoke:

8. 'Whatever pain arises is all in consequence of the samkhâras, by the destruction of the samkhâras there will be no origin of pain. (731)

9. 'Looking upon this pain that springs from the samkhâras as misery, from the cessation of all the samkhâras, and from the destruction of consciousness will arise the destruction of pain, having understood this exactly, (732)

10. 'The wise who have true views and are accomplished, having understood (all things) completely, and having

218

conquered all association with Mâra, do not go to re-birth. (733)

'"Should there be a perfect consideration of the Dyad in another way," if, O Bhikkhus, there are people that ask so, they shall be told, there is, and how there is: "Whatever pain arises is all in consequence of viññâna (consciousness)," this is one consideration, "but from the complete destruction of viññânana, through absence of passion, there is no origin of pain," this is the second consideration; thus, O Bhikkhus, by the Bhikkhu that considers the Dyad duly, that is strenuous, ardent, resolute, of two fruits one fruit is to be expected: in this world perfect knowledge, or, if any of the (five) attributes still remain, the state of an Anâgâmin (one that does not return).' This said Bhagavat, (and) when Sugata had said this, the Master further spoke:

11. 'Whatever pain arises is all in consequence of viññâna, by the destruction of viññâna there is no origin of pain. (734)

p. 136

12. 'Looking upon this pain that springs from viññâna as misery, from the cessation of viññâna a Bhikkhu free from desire (will be) perfectly happy (parinibbuta). (735)

'"Should there be a perfect consideration of the Dyad in

219

another way," if, O Bhikkhus, there are people that ask so, they shall be told, there is, and how there is: "Whatever pain arises is all in consequence of phassa (touch)," this is one consideration, "but from the complete destruction of phassa, through absence of passion, there is no origin of pain," this is the second consideration; thus, O Bhikkhus, by the Bhikkhu that considers the Dyad duly, that is strenuous, ardent, resolute, of two fruits one fruit is to be expected: in this world perfect knowledge, or, if any of the (five) attributes still remain, the state of an Anâgâmin (one that does not return).' This said Bhagavat, (and) when Sugata had said this, the Master further spoke:

13. 'For those who are ruined by phassa, who follow the stream of existence, who have entered a bad way, the destruction of bonds is far off. (736)

14. 'But those who, having fully understood phassa, knowingly have taken delight in cessation, they verily from the comprehension of phassa, and being free from desire, are perfectly happy. (737)

'"Should there be a perfect consideration of the Dyad in another way," if, O Bhikkhus, there are people that ask so, they shall be told, there is, and how there is: "Whatever pain arises is all in consequence of the vedanâs (sensations)," this is one consideration, "but from the complete destruction of the vedanâs, through absence of passion, there no origin of pain," this is the second consideration; thus, O Bhikkhus, by the Bhikkhu that considers the Dyad duly, that is strenuous, ardent, resolute, of two fruits one fruit is to be expected: in this world perfect knowledge, or, if any of the (five) attributes still remain, the state of an Anâgâmin (one that does not return).' This said Bhagavat, (and) when Sugata had said this, the Master further spoke:

15. 'Pleasure or pain, together with want of pleasure and want of pain, whatever is perceived internally and externally, (738)

16. 'Looking upon this as pain, having touched what is perishable and fragile, seeing the decay (of everything), the Bhikkhu is disgusted, having from the perishing of the vedanâs become free from desire, and perfectly happy. (739)

'"Should there be a perfect consideration of the Dyad in another way," if, O Bhikkhus, there are people that ask so, they shall be told, there is, and how there is: "Whatever pain arises is all in consequence of tanhâ (desire)," this is one consideration, "but from the complete destruction of tanhâ, through absence of passion, there is no origin of pain," this is the second consideration; thus, O Bhikkhus, by the Bhikkhu that considers the Dyad duly, that is strenuous, ardent, resolute, of two fruits one fruit is to be expected: in this world perfect knowledge, or, if any of the (five) attributes still remain, the state of an Anâgâmin (one that does not return).' This said Bhagavat, (and) when Sugata had said this, the Master further spoke:

17. 'A man accompanied by tanhâ, for a long time transmigrating into existence in this way or

p. 138

that way, does not overcome transmigration (samsâra). (740)

18. 'Looking upon this as misery, this origin of the pain of tanhâ, let the Bhikkhu free from tanhâ, not seizing (upon anything), thoughtful, wander about. (741)

'"Should there be a perfect consideration of the Dyad in another way," if, O Bhikkhus, there are people that ask so, they shall be told, there is, and how there is: "Whatever pain arises is all in consequence of the upâdânas (the seizures)," this is one consideration, "but from the complete destruction of the upâdânas, through absence of passion, there is no origin of pain," this is the second consideration; thus, O Bhikkhus, by the Bhikkhu that considers the Dyad duly, that is strenuous, ardent, resolute, of two fruits one fruit is to be expected: in this world perfect knowledge, or, if any of the (five) attributes still remain, the state of an Anâgâmin (one that does not return).' This said Bhagavat, (and) when Sugata had said this, the Master further spoke:

19. 'The existence is in consequence of the upâdânas; he who has come into existence goes to pain, he who has been born is to die, this is the origin of pain. (742)

20. 'Therefore from the destruction of the upâdânas the wise with perfect knowledge, having seen (what causes) the destruction of birth, do not go to re-birth. (743)

'"Should there be a perfect consideration of the Dyad in another way," if, O Bhikkhus, there are people that ask so, they shall be told, there is, and how there is: "Whatever pain arises is all in

p. 139

consequence of the ârambhas (exertions)," this is one consideration, "but from the complete destruction of the ârambhas, through absence of passion, there is no origin of pain," this is the second consideration; thus, O Bhikkhus, by the Bhikkhu that considers the Dyad duly, that is strenuous, ardent, resolute, of two fruits one fruit is to be expected: in this world perfect knowledge, or, if any of the (five) attributes still remain, the state of an Anâgâmin (one that does not return).' This said Bhagavat, (and) when Sugata had said this, the Master further spoke:

21. 'Whatever pain arises is all in consequence of the ârambhas, by the destruction of the ârambhas there is no origin of pain. (744)

22, 23. 'Looking upon this pain that springs from the ârambhas as misery, having abandoned all the ârambhas, birth and transmigration have been crossed over by the Bhikkhu who is liberated in non-exertion, who has cut off the desire for existence, and whose mind is calm; there is for him no re-birth. (745, 746)

'"Should there be a perfect consideration of the Dyad in another way," if, O Bhikkhus, there are people that ask so, they shall be told, there is, and how there is: "Whatever pain arises is all in consequence of the âhâras (food?)," this is one consideration, "but from the complete destruction of the âhâras, through absence of passion, there is no origin of pain," this is the second consideration; thus, O Bhikkhus, by the Bhikkhu that considers the Dyad duly, that is strenuous, ardent, resolute, of two fruits one fruit is to be expected: in this world perfect knowledge, or, if any of the (five) attributes still

p. 140

remain, the state of an Anâgâmin (one that does not return).'

This said Bhagavat, (and) when Sugata had said this, the Master further spoke:

24. 'Whatever pain arises is all in consequence of the âhâras, by the destruction of the âhâras there is no origin of pain. (747)

25. 'Looking upon this pain that springs from the âhâras as misery, having seen the result of all âhâras, not resorting to all âhâras, (748)

26. 'Having seen that health is from the destruction of desire, he that serves discriminatingly and stands fast in the Dhamma cannot be reckoned as existing, being accomplished[1]. (749)

'"Should there be a perfect consideration of the Dyad in another way," if, O Bhikkhus, there are people that ask so, they shall be told, there is, and how there is: "Whatever pain arises is all in consequence of the iñgitas (commotions)," this is one consideration, "but from the complete destruction of the iñgitas, through absence of passion, there is no origin of pain," this is the second consideration; thus, O Bhikkhus, by the Bhikkhu that considers the Dyad duly, that is strenuous, ardent, resolute, of two fruits one fruit is to be expected: in this world perfect knowledge, or, if any of the (five) attributes still remain, the state of an Anâgâmin (one that does not return).' This said Bhagavat, (and) when Sugata had said this, the Master further spoke:

27. 'Whatever pain arises is all in consequence of the iñgitas, by the destruction of the iñgitas there is no origin of pain. (750)

28. 'Looking upon this pain that springs from

[1. Samkham nôpeti vedagû.]

p. 141

the iñgitas as misery, and therefore having abandoned the iñgitas and having stopped the samkhâras; let the Bhikkhu free from desire and not seizing (upon anything), thoughtful, wander about. (751)

'"Should there be a perfect consideration of the Dyad in another way," if, O Bhikkhus, there are people that ask so, they shall be told, there is, and how there is: "For the nissita (dependent) there is vacillation," this is one consideration, "the independent (man) does not vacillate," this is the second consideration; thus, O Bhikkhus, by the Bhikkhu that considers the Dyad duly, that is strenuous, ardent, resolute, of two fruits one fruit is to be expected: in this world perfect knowledge, or, if any of the (five) attributes still remain, the state of an Anâgâmin (one that does not return).' This said Bhagavat, (and) when Sugata had said this, the Master further spoke:

29. 'The independent (man) does not vacillate, and the dependent (man) seizing upon existence in one way or in another, does not overcome samsâra. (752).

30. 'Looking upon this as misery (and seeing) great danger in things you depend upon, let a Bhikkhu wander about independent, not seizing (upon anything), thoughtful. (753)

'"Should there be a perfect consideration of the Dyad in another way," if, O Bhikkhus, there are people that ask so, they shall be told, there is, and how there is: "The formless (beings), O Bhikkhus, are calmer than the rûpas (for ruppa, i.e. form-possessing)," this is one consideration, "cessation is calmer than the formless," this is another consideration, "thus, O Bhikkhus, by the Bhikkhu that considers

p. 142

the Dyad duly, that is strenuous, ardent, resolute, of two fruits one fruit is to be expected: in this world perfect knowledge, or, if any of the (five) attributes still remain, the state of an Anâgâmin (one that does not return).' This said Bhagavat, (and) when Sugata had said this, the Master further spoke:

31. 'Those beings who are possessed of form, and those who dwell in the formless (world), not knowing cessation, have to go to re-birth. (754)

32. 'But those who, having fully comprehended the forms, stand fast in the formless (worlds), those who are liberated in the cessation, such beings leave death behind. (755)

'"Should there be a perfect consideration of the Dyad in another way," if, O Bhikkhus, there are people that ask so, they shall be told, there is, and how there is: "What has been considered true by the world of men, together with the gods, Mâra, Brahman, and amongst the Samanas, Brâmanas, gods, and men, that has by the noble through their perfect knowledge been well seen to be really false," this is one consideration; "what, O Bhikkhus, has been considered false by the world of men, together with the gods, Mâra, Brahman, and amongst the Samanas, Brâmanas, gods, and men, that has by the noble through their perfect knowledge been well seen to be really true," this is another consideration. Thus, O Bhikkhus, by the Bhikkhu that considers the Dyad duly, that is strenuous, ardent, resolute, of two fruits one fruit is to be expected: in this world perfect knowledge, or, if any of the (five) attributes still remain, the state of an Anâgâmin (one that does not return).' This said Bhagavat,

p. 143

(and) when Sugata had said this, the Master further spoke:

33. 'Seeing the real in the unreal, the world of men and gods dwelling in name and form[1], he thinks: "This is true." (756)

34. 'Whichever way they think (it), it becomes otherwise, for it is false to him, and what is false is perishable[2]. (?) (757)

35. 'What is not false, the Nibbâna, that the noble conceive as true, they verily from the comprehension of truth are free from desire (and) perfectly happy[3]. (758)

"'Should there be a perfect consideration of the Dyad in another way," if, O Bhikkhus, there are people that ask so, they shall be told, there is, and how there is: "What, O Bhikkhus, has been considered pleasure by the world of men, gods, Mâra, Brahman, and amongst the Samanas, Brâmanas, gods, and men, that has by the noble by (their) perfect knowledge been well seen to be really pain," this is one consideration; "what, O Bhikkhus, has been considered pain by the world of men, gods, Mâra, Brahman, and amongst the Samanas, Brâhmanas, gods, and men, that has by the noble by their perfect knowledge been well seen to be really pleasure," this is the second consideration. Thus, O

[1. Nâmarûpasmim, 'individuality.'

2. Yena yena hi maññanti
Tato tam hoti aññathâ,
Tam hi tassa musâ hoti,
Mosadhammam hi ittaram.

3. Amosadhammam nibbânam
Tad ariyâ sakkato vidû,
Te ye sakkâbhisamayâ
Nikkhâtâ parinibbutâ.]

p. 144

Bhikkhus, by the Bhikkhu who considers the Dyad duly, who is strenuous, ardent, resolute, of two fruits one fruit is to be expected: in this world perfect knowledge, or, if any of the (five) attributes still remain, the state of an Anâgâmin (one who does not return).' This said Bhagavat, (and) when Sugata had said so, the Master further spoke:

36. 'Form, sound, taste, smell, and touch are all wished for, pleasing and charming (things) as long as they last, so it is said. (759)

37. 'By you, by the world of men and gods these (things) are deemed a pleasure, but when they cease it is deemed pain by

230

them. (760)

38. 'By the noble the cessation of the existing body is regarded as pleasure; this is the opposite of (what) the wise in all the world (hold)[1]. (761)

39. 'What fools say is pleasure that the noble say is pain, what fools say is pain that the noble know as pleasure:--see here is a thing difficult to understand, here the ignorant are confounded. (762)

40. 'For those that are enveloped there is gloom, for those that do not see there is darkness, and for the good it is manifest, for those that see there is light; (even being) near, those that are ignorant of the way and the Dhamma, do not discern (anything) [2]. (763)

[1. Sukhan ti dittham ariyehi
Sakkâyass' uparodhanam,
Pakkanîkam idam hoti
Sabbalokena passatam.

2. Nivutânam tamo hotî
Andhakâro apassatam,
Satañ ka vivatam hoti
Âloko passatâm iva,

Santike na vigânanti
Magadhammass' akovidâ.]

p. 145

41. 'By those that are overcome by the passions of existence, by those that follow the stream of existence, by those that have entered the realm of Mâra, this Dhamma is not perfectly understood. (764)

42. 'Who except the noble deserve the well-understood state (of Nibbâna)? Having perfectly conceived this state, those free from passion are completely extinguished[1].' (765)

This spoke Bhagavat. Glad those Bhikkhus rejoiced at the words of Bhagavat. While this explanation was being given, the minds of sixty Bhikkhus, not seizing (upon anything), were liberated.

Dvayatânupassanâsutta is ended.

Mahâvagga, the third.

[1. Ko nu aññatra-m-ariyehi
Padam sambuddham arahati

Yam padam samma-d-aññâya
Parinibbanti anâsavâ.]

IV. ATTHAKAVAGGA.

1. KÂMASUTTA.

Sensual pleasures are to be avoided.

1. If he who desires sensual pleasures is successful, he certainly becomes glad-minded, having obtained what a mortal wishes for. (766)

2. But if those sensual pleasures fail the person who desires and wishes (for them), he will suffer, pierced by the arrow (of pain). (767)

3. He who avoids sensual pleasures as (he would avoid treading upon) the head of a snake with his foot, such a one, being thoughtful (sato), will conquer this desire. (768)

4. He who covets extensively (such) pleasures (as these), fields, goods, or gold, cows and horses, servants, women, relations, (769)

5. Sins will overpower him, dangers will crush him, and pain will follow him as water (pours into) a broken ship. (770)

6. Therefore let one always be thoughtful, and avoid pleasures; having abandoned them, let him cross the stream, after baling out the ship, and go to the other shore. (771)

Kâmasutta is ended.

p. 147

2. GUHATTHAKASUTTA.

Let no one cling to existence and sensual pleasures.
1. A man that lives adhering to the cave (i.e. the body), who is covered with much (sin), and sunk into delusion, such a one is far from seclusion, for the sensual pleasures in the world are not easy to abandon. (772)

2. Those whose wishes are their motives, those who are linked to the pleasures of the world, they are difficult to liberate, for they cannot be liberated by others, looking for what is after or what is before, coveting these and former sensual pleasures. (773)

3. Those who are greedy of, given to, and infatuated by sensual pleasures, those who are niggardly, they, having entered upon what is wicked, wail when they are subjected to pain, saying: 'What will become of us, when we die away from here?' (774)

4. Therefore let a man here[1] learn, whatever he knows as wicked in the world, let him not for the sake of that (?) practise (what is) wicked[2]; for short is this life, say the wise. (775)

5. I see in the world this trembling race given to desire for existences; they are wretched men who lament in the mouth of death, not being free from the desire for reiterated existences. (776)

6. Look upon those men trembling in selfishness, like fish in a stream nearly dried up, with little water; seeing this, let one wander about unselfish, without forming any attachment to existences. (777)

[1. Idheva = imasmim yeva sâsane. Commentator.

2. Na tassa hetu visamam kareyya.]

p. 148

7. Having subdued his wish for both ends[1], having fully understood touch without being greedy, not doing what he has himself blamed, the wise (man) does not cling to what is seen and heard[2]. (778)

8. Having understood name[3], let the Muni cross over the stream, not defiled by any grasping; having pulled out the arrow (of passion), wandering about strenuous, he does not wish for this world or the other. (779)

Guhatthakasutta is ended.

3. DUTTHATTHAKASUTTA.

The Muni undergoes no censure, for he has shaken off all systems of philosophy, and is therefore independent.
1. Verily, some wicked-minded people censure, and also just-minded people censure, but the Muni does not undergo the censure that has arisen; therefore there is not a discontented (khila) Muni anywhere. (780)

2. How can he who is led by his wishes and possessed by his inclinations overcome his own (false) view? Doing his own doings let him talk according to his understanding[4]. (781)

3. The person who, without being asked, praises

[1. Comp. Sallasutta, v. 9.

2. Ubhosu antesu vineyya khandam
Phassam pariññâya anânugiddho
Yad atta garahî tad akubbamâno
Na lippatî ditthasutesu dhîro.

3. Saññam = nâmarûpam. Commentator.

4. Sakam hi ditthim katham akkayeyya
Khandânunîto rukiyâ nivittho,
Sayam samattâni pakubbamâno
Yathâ hi gâneyya tathâ vadeyya.]

p. 149

his own virtue and (holy) works to others, him the good call
ignoble, one who praises himself[1]. (782)

4. But the Bhikkhu who is calm and of a happy mind, thus not
praising himself for his virtues, him the good call noble, one for

whom there are no desires anywhere in the world[2]. (783)

5. He whose Dhammas are (arbitrarily) formed and fabricated, placed in front, and confused, because he sees in himself a good result, is therefore given to (the view which is called) kuppa-patikka-santi[3]. (?) (784)

6. For the dogmas of philosophy are not easy to overcome, amongst the Dhammas (now this and now that) is adopted after consideration; therefore a man rejects and adopts (now this and now that) Dhamma amongst the dogmas[4]. (785)

7. For him who has shaken off (sin) there is nowhere in the world any prejudiced view of the different existences; he who has shaken off (sin), after leaving deceit and arrogance behind, which (way) should he go, he (is) independent[6]. (786)

[1. Yo âtumânam sayam eva pâvâ = yo evam attânam sayam eva vadati. Commentator.

2. Yass' ussadâ n' atthi kuhiñki loke.

3. Pakappitâ samkhatâ yassa dhammâ
Purakkhatâ santi avîvadâtâ
Yad attanî passati ânisamsam
Tam nissito kuppapatikkasantim.

4. Ditthînivesâ na hi svâtivattâ,
Dhammesu nikkheyya samuggahîtam,
Tasmâ naro tesu nivesanesu
Nirassatî âdiyati-kka dhammam.
Comp. Paramatthakasutta, v. 6.

5. Dhonassa hî n' atthi kuhiñki loke
Pakappitâ ditthi bhavâbhavesu,
Mâyañ ka mânañ ka pahâya dhono
Sa kena gakkheyya, anûpayo so.]

p. 150

8. But he who is dependent undergoes censure amongst the Dhammas; with what (name) and how should one name him who is independent? For by him there is nothing grasped or rejected, he has in this world shaken off every (philosophical) view[1]. (787)

Dutthatthakasutta is ended.

4. SUDDHATTHAKASUTTA.

No one is purified by philosophy, those devoted to philosophy run from one teacher to another, but the wise are not led by passion, and do not embrace anything in the world as the highest.

1. I see a pure, most excellent, sound man, by his views a man's purification takes place, holding this opinion, and having seen this view to be the highest he goes back to knowledge, thinking to see what is pure[2]. (788)

2. If a man's purification takes place by (his philosophical) views, or he by knowledge leaves pain behind, then he is purified by another (way than the ariyamagga, i.e. the noble way), together with his upadhis, on account of his views he tells him to say so[3]. (789)

[1. Upayo[*] hi dhammesu upeti vâdam
Anûpayam kena katham vadeyya
Attam nirattam na hi tassa atthi
Adhosi so ditthim idh' eva sabbam.

2. Passâmi suddham paramam arogam,
Ditthena samsuddhi narassa hoti,
Et' âbhigânam paraman ti ñatvâ.
Suddhânupassiti pakketi ñânam.

3. Ditthîhi nam pâva tathâ vadânam.
Comp. Garâsutta, v. l0; Pasûrasutta, v. 7.

*. Upayo ti tanhâditthinissito. Commentator.]

p. 151

3. But the Brâhmana who does not cling to what has been seen, or heard, to virtue and (holy) works, or to what has been thought, to what is good and to what is evil, and who leaves behind what has been grasped, without doing anything in this world, he does not acknowledge that purification cornes from another[1]. (790)

4. Having left (their) former (teacher) they go to another, following their desires they do not break asunder their ties; they grasp, they let go like a monkey letting go the branch (just) after having caught (hold of it). (791)

5. Having himself undertaken some (holy) works he goes to various (things) led by his senses, but a man of great understanding, a wise man who by his wisdom has understood the Dhamma, does not go to various (occupations). (792)

6. He being secluded amongst all the Dhammas, whatever has been seen, heard, or thought--how should any one in this world be able to alter him, the seeing one, who wanders openly[2]? (793)

7. They do not form (any view), they do not prefer (anything), they do not say, 'I am infinitely pure;' having cut the tied knot of attachment, they do not long for (anything) anywhere in the world. (794)

[1.Na brâhmano aññato suddhim âha
Ditthe sute sîlavate mute vâ
puññe ka pâpe ka anûpalitto
Attañgaho na idha pakubbamâno.

2. Sa sabbadhammesu visenibhûto[*]
Yam kiñki dittham va sutam mutam vâ
Tam eva dassim vivatam karantam
Ken' îdha lokasmim vikappayeyya?

*.   Mârasenam   vinâsetvâ   thitabhâvena   visenibhûto.
Commentator.]

p. 152

8. He is a Brâhmana that has conquered (sin)[1]; by him there is nothing embraced after knowing and seeing it; he is not affected by any kind of passion; there is nothing grasped by him as the highest in this world. (795)

Suddhatthakasutta is ended.

5. PARAMATTHAKASUTTA.

One should not give oneself to philosophical disputations; a Brâhmana who does not adopt any system of philosophy, is unchangeable, has reached Nibbâna.
1. What one person, abiding by the (philosophical) views, saying, 'This is the most excellent,' considers the highest in the world, everything different from that he says is wretched, therefore he has not overcome dispute[2]. (796)

2. Because he sees in himself a good result, with regard to what has been seen (or) heard, virtue and (holy) works, or what has been thought, therefore, having embraced that, he looks upon everything else as bad[3]. (797)

3. The expert call just that a tie dependent

[1. Katunnam kilesasîmânam atîtattâ
Sîmâtigo bâhitapâpattâ ka brâhmano.

2. Paraman ti ditthîsu paribbasâno
Yad uttarim kurute gantu loke

244

Hînâ ti aññe tato sabbam âha,
Tasmâ vivâdâni avîtivatto.
Properly, 'others (are) wretched.'

3. Yad attanî passati ânisamsam
Ditthe sute sîlavate mute vâ
Tad eva so tattha samuggahâya
Nihînato passati sabbam aññam.]

p. 153

upon which one looks upon anything else as bad. Therefore let
a Bhikkhu not depend upon what is seen, heard, or thought, or
upon virtue and (holy) works[1]. (798)

4. Let him not form any (philosophical) view in this world,
either by knowledge or by virtue and (holy) works, let him not
represent himself equal (to others), nor think himself either low
or distinguished. (799)

5. Having left what has been grasped, not seizing upon
anything he does not depend even on knowledge. He does not
associate with those that are taken up by different things, he
does not return to any (philosophical) view[2]. (800)

6. For whom there is here no desire for both ends, for

reiterated existence either here or in another world, for him there are no resting-places (of the mind) embraced after investigation amongst the doctrines (dhammesu)[3]. (801)

7. In him there is not the least prejudiced idea with regard to what has been seen, heard, or thought; how could any one in this world alter such a Brâhmana who does not adopt any view? (802)

[1. Tam vâpi gantham kusalâ vadanti
Yam nissito passati hînam aññam,
Tasmâ hi dittham va sutam mutam vâ
Sîlabbatam bhikkhu na nissayeyya.

2. Attam pahâya anupâdiyâno
Ñâne pi so nissayam no karoti,
Sa ve viyattesu na vaggasârî,
Ditthim pi so na pakketi kiñki.

3. Yass' ûbhayante panidhîdha n' atthi
Bhavâbhavâya idha vâ huram vâ
Nivesanâ tassa na santi keki
Dhammesu nikkheyya samuggahîtâ.]

p. 154

8. They do not form (any view), they do not prefer (anything), the Dhammas are not chosen by them, a Brâhmana is not dependent upon virtue and (holy) works; having gone to the other shore, such a one does not return. (803)

Paramatthakasutta is ended.

6. GARÂSUTTA.

From selfishness come grief and avarice; The Bhikkhu who has turned away frorn the world and wanders about houseless, is independent, and does not wish for purification through another.

1. Short indeed is this life, within a hundred years one dies, and if any one lives longer, then he dies of old age. (804)

2. People grieve from selfishness, perpetual cares kill them, this (world) is full of disappointment; seeing this, let one not live in a house. (805)

3. That even of which a man thinks 'this is mine' is left behind by death: knowing this, let not the wise (man) turn himself to worldliness (while being my) follower[1]. (806)

4. As a man awakened does not see what he has met with in his

sleep, so also he does not see the beloved person that has passed away and is dead. (807)

5. Both seen and heard are the persons whose particular name is mentioned, but only the name

[1. Maranena pi tam pahîyati
Yam puriso mama-y-idan ti maññati,
Evam pi viditvâ pandito
Na pamattâya nametha mâmako.]

p. 155

remains undecayed of the person that has passed away[1]. (808)

6. The greedy in their selfishness do not leave sorrow, lamentation, and avarice; therefore the Munis leaving greediness wandered about seeing security (i.e. Nibbâna). (809)

7. For a Bhikkhu, who wanders about unattached and cultivates the mind of a recluse, they say it is proper that he does not show himself (again) in existence[2]. (810)

8. Under all circumstances the independent Muni does not

please nor displease (any one); sorrow and avarice do not stick to him (as little) as water to a leaf. (811)

9. As a drop of water does not stick to a lotus, as water does not stick to a lotus, so a Muni does not cling to anything, namely, to what is seen or heard or thought[3]. (812)

10. He who has shaken off (sin) does not therefore think (much of anything) because it has been seen or heard or thought; he does not wish for

[1. Ditthâpi sutâpi te ganâ
Yesam nâmam idam pavukkati
Nâmam evâvasissati
Akkheyyam petassa gantuno.

2. Patilînakarassa bhikkhuno
Bhagamânassa vittamânasam[*]
Sâmaggiyam âhu tassa tam
Yo attânam bhavane na dassaye.

3. Udabindu yathâpi pokkhare
Padume vâri yathâ na lippati
Evam muni nôpalippati
Yad idam dittthasutam mutesu vâ.

*. Bi has vivitta-.]

p. 156

purification through another, for he is not pleased nor displeased (with anything)[1]. (813)

Garâsutta is ended.

7. TISSAMETTEYYASUTTA.

Sexual intercourse should be avoided.
1. 'Tell me, O venerable one,'--so said the venerable Tissa Metteyya,--'the defeat of him who is given to sexual intercourse; hearing thy precepts we will learn in seclusion.' (814)

2. 'The precepts of him who is given to sexual intercourse, O Metteyya,'--so said Bhagavat,--'are lost, and he employs himself wrongly, this is what is ignoble in him. (815)

3. 'He who, having formerly wandered alone, gives himself up to sexual intercourse, him they call in the world a low, common fellow, like a rolling chariot. (816)

4. 'What honour and renown he had before, that is lost for him; having seen this let him learn to give up sexual intercourse. (817)

5. 'He who overcome by his thoughts meditates like a miser, such a one, having heard the (blaming) voice of others, becomes discontented. (818)

6. 'Then he makes weapons (i.e. commits evil

[1. Dhono na hi tena maññati
Yad idam ditthasutam mutesu vâ,
Nâññena visuddhim ikkhati,
Na hi so raggati no viraggati.
Comp. Suddhatthakasutta, v. 2.]

p. 157

deeds) urged by the doctrines of others, he is very greedy, and sinks into falsehood[1]. (819)

7. 'Designated "wise" he has entered upon a solitary life, then having given himself up to sexual intercourse, he (being) a fool suffers pain. (820)

8. 'Looking upon this as misery let the Muni from first to last in the world firmly keep to his solitary life, let him not give himself up to sexual intercourse. (821)

9. 'Let him learn seclusion, this is the highest for noble men, but let him not therefore think himself the best, although he is verily near Nibbâna. (822)

10. 'The Muni who wanders void (of desire), not coveting sensual pleasures, and who has crossed the stream, him the creatures that are tied in sensual pleasures envy.' (823)

Tissametteyyasutta is ended.

8. PASÛRASUTTA.

Disputants brand each other as fools, they wish for praise, but being repulsed they become discontented; one is not purified by dispute, but by keeping to Buddha, who has shaken off all sin.
1. Here they maintain 'purity,' in other doctrines (dhamma) they do not allow purity; what they have devoted themselves to, that they call good, and they enter extensively upon the single truths[2]. (824)

[1. Atha satthâni kurute
Paravâdehi kodito,
Esa khv-assa mahâgedho,
Mosavaggam pagâhati.

2. Idh' eya suddhim iti vâdiyanti
Nâññesu dhammesu visuddhim âhu
Yam nissitâ tattha subham vadânâ
Pakkekasakkesu puthû nivitthâ.]

p. 158

2. Those wishing for dispute, having plunged into the assembly, brand each other as fools mutually, they go to others and pick a quarrel, wishing for praise and calling themselves (the only) expert. (825)

3. Engaged in dispute in the middle of the assembly, wishing for praise he lays about on all sides; but when his dispute has been repulsed he becomes discontented, at the blame he gets angry he who sought for the faults (of others). (826)

4. Because those who have tested his questions say that his dispute is lost and repulsed, he laments and grieves having lost his disputes; 'he has conquered me,' so saying he wails. (827)

5. These disputes have arisen amongst the Samanas, in these (disputes) there is (dealt) blow (and) stroke; having seen this, let him leave off disputing, for there is no other advantage in trying to get praise. (828)

6. Or he is praised there, having cleared up the dispute in the middle of the assembly; therefore he will laugh and be elated, having won that case as he had a mind to. (829)

7. That which is his exaltation will also be the field of his defeat, still he talks proudly and arrogantly; seeing this, let no one dispute, for the expert do not say that purification (takes place) by that[1]. (830)

8. As a hero nourished by kingly food goes about roaring, wishing for an adversary--where he (i.e. the philosopher, Ditthigatika) is, go thou there, O

[1. Yi unnatî sâssa vighâtabûmi,
Mânâtimânam vadate pan' eso,
Etam pi disvâ na vivâdayetha
Na hi tena suddhim kusalâ vadanti.
Comp. Suddhatthakasutta, v. 2.]

hero; formerly there was nothing like this to fight against[1]. (831)

9. Those who, having embraced a (certain philosophical) view, dispute and maintain 'this only (is) true,' to them say thou when a dispute has arisen, 'Here is no opponent[2] for thee.' (832)

10. Those who wander about after having secluded themselves, without opposing view to view--what (opposition) wilt thou meet with amongst those, O Pasûra, by whom nothing in this world is grasped as the best? (833)

11. Then thou wentest to reflection thinking in thy mind over the (different philosophical) views; thou hast gone into the yoke with him who has shaken off (all sin), but thou wilt not be able to proceed together (with him)[3]. (834)

Pasûrasutta is ended.

9. MÂGANDIYASUTTA.

A dialogue between Mâgandiya and Buddha. The former offers Buddha his daughter for a wife, but Buddha refuses her.

Mâgandiya says that purity cornes from philosophy, Buddha from 'inward peace.' The Muni is a confessor of peace, he does not dispute, he is free from marks.

1. Buddha: 'Even seeing Tanhâ, Arati, and Ragâ (the daughters of Mâra), there was not the least wish

[1. Sûro yathâ râgakhâdâya puttho
Abhigaggam eti patisûram ikkham--
Yen' eva so tena palehi sûra,
Pubbe va n' atthi yad idam yudhâya.

2. Patisenikattâ ti patilomakârako. Commentator.

3. Atha tvam pavitakkam âgamâ
Manasâ ditthigatâni kintayanto,
Dhonena yugam samâgamâ,
Na hi tvam pagghasi sampayâtave.]

p. 160

(in me) for sexual intercourse. What is this (thy daughter's body but a thing) full of water and excrement? I do not even want to touch it with my foot.' (835)

2. Mâgandiya: 'If thou dost not want such a pearl, a woman

desired by many kings, what view, virtue, and (holy) works, (mode of) life, re-birth dost thou profess?' (836)

3. '"This I say," so (I do now declare), after investigation there is nothing amongst the doctrines which such a one (as I would) embrace, O Mâgandiya,'-- so said Bhagavat,--'and seeing (misery) in the (philosophical) views, without adopting (any of them), searching (for truth) I saw "inward peace[1]."' (837)

4. 'All the (philosophical) resolutions[2] that have been formed,'--so said Mâgandiya,--'those indeed thou explainest without adopting (any of them); the notion "inward peace" which (thou mentionest), how is this explained by the wise?' (838)

5. 'Not by (any philosophical) opinion, not by tradition, not by knowledge, O Mâgandiya,'--so said Bhagavat,--'not by virtue and (holy) works can any one say that purity exists; nor by absence of (philosophical) opinion, by absence of tradition, by absence of knowledge, by absence of virtue and (holy) works either; having abandoned these without adopting (anything else), let him, calm and independent, not desire existence[3]. (839)

[1. Idam vadâmîti na tassa hoti--Mâgandiyâ ti Bhagavâ--
Dhammesu nikkheyya samuggahîtam
Passañ ka ditthîsu anuggahâya
Agghattasantim pakinam adassam.

2. Vinikkhaya, placita?

3. Na ditthiyâ na sutiyâ na ñânena--Mâgandiyâ ti Bhagavâ--
Sîlabbatenâpi na suddhim âha
Aditthiyâ assutiyâ aññânâ
Asîlatâ abbatâ no pi tena,
Ete ka nissagga anuggahâya
Santo anissâya bhavam na gappe.]

p. 161

6. 'If one cannot say by (any philosophical) opinion, or by
tradition, or by knowledge,'--so said Mâgandiya,--'or by virtue
and (holy) works that purity exists, nor by absence of
(philosophical) opinion, by absence of tradition, by absence of
knowledge, by absence of virtue and (holy) works, then I
consider the doctrine foolish, for by (philosophical) opinions
some return to purity.' (840)

7. 'And asking on account of (thy philosophical) opinion, O
Mâgandiya,'--so said Bhagavat,--'thou hast gone to infatuation
in what thou hast embraced, and of this (inward peace) thou
hast not the least idea, therefore thou holdest it foolish[1]. (841)

8. 'He who thinks himself equal (to others), or distinguished, or low, he for that very reason disputes; but he who is unmoved under those three conditions, for him (the notions) "equal" and "distinguished" do not exist. (842)

9. 'The Brâhmana for whom (the notions) "equal" and "unequal" do not exist, would he say, "This is true?" Or with whom should he dispute, saying, "This is false?" With whom should he enter into dispute[2]? (843)

10. 'Having left his house, wandering about

[1. Ditthiñ ka nissâya anupukkhamâno
Samuggahîtesu pamoham âgâ
Ito ka nâddakkhi anum pi saññam
Tasmâ tuvam momuhato dahâsi.

2. Sakkan ti so brâhmano kim vadeyya
Musâ ti vâ so vivadetha kena
Yasmim samam visamañ kâpi n' atthi
Sa kena vâdam patisamyugeyya.]

p. 162

houseless, not making acquaintances in the village, free from lust, not desiring (any future existence), let the Muni not get

259

into quarrelsome talk with people. (844)

11. 'Let not an eminent man (nâga) dispute after having embraced those (views) separated from which he (formerly) wandered in the world; as the thorny lotus elambuga is undefiled by water and mud, so the Muni, the confessor of peace, free from greed, does not cling to sensual pleasures and the world. (845)

12. 'An accomplished man does not by (a philosophical) view, or by thinking become arrogant, for he is not of that sort; not by (holy) works, nor by tradition is he to be led, he is not led into any of the resting-places (of the mind). (846)

13. 'For him who is free from marks there are no ties, to him who is delivered by understanding there are no follies; (but those) who grasped after marks and (philosophical) views, they wander about in the world annoying (people)[1].' (847)

Mâgandiyasutta is ended.

10. PURÂBHEDASUTTA.

Definition of a calm Muni.
1. 'With what view and with what virtue is one called calm, tell

me that, O Gotama, (when) asked about the best man?' (848)

2. 'He whose desire is departed before the dissolution (of his body),'--so said Bhagavat,--'who

[1. Saññâvirattassa na santi ganthâ,
Paññâvimuttassa na santi mohâ,
Saññañ ka ditthiñ ka ye aggahesum
Te ghattayantâ vikaranti loke.]

p. 163

does not depend upon beginning and end, nor reckons upon the middle, by him there is nothing preferred[1]. (849)

3. 'He who is free from anger, free from trembling, free from boasting, free from misbehaviour, he who speaks wisely, he who is not elated, he is indeed a Muni who has restrained his speech. (850)

4. 'Without desire for the future he does not grieve for the past, he sees seclusion in the phassas (touch), and he is not led by (any philosophical) views. (851)

5. 'He is unattached, not deceitful, not covetous, not envious,

not impudent, not contemptuous, and not given to slander. (852)

6. 'Without desire for pleasant things and not given to conceit, and being gentle, intelligent, not credulous, he is not displeased (with anything). (853)

7. 'Not from love of gain does he learn, and he does not get angry on account of loss, and untroubled by desire he has no greed for sweet things[2]. (854)

8. 'Equable (upekhaka), always thoughtful, he does not think himself equal (to others)[3] in the world, nor distinguished, nor low: for him there are no desires (ussada). (855)

[1. Vîtatanho purâ bhedâ
Pubbam antam anissito
Vemagghe n' ûpasamkheyyo
Tassa n' atthi purekkhatam.

2. Rasesu nânugigghati

3. Na loke maññate samam
Na visesî na nîkeyyo.
Compare Tuvatakasutta, v. 4; Attadandasutta, v. 20.]

9. 'The man for whom there is nothing upon which he depends, who is independent, having understood the Dhamma, for whom there is no desire for coming into existence or leaving existence, (856)

10. 'Him I call calm, not looking for sensual pleasures; for him there are no ties, he has overcome desire. (857)

11. 'For him there are no sons, cattle, fields, wealth, nothing grasped or rejected is to be found in him, (858)

12. 'That fault of which common people and Samanas and Brâhmanas say that he is possessed, is not possessed by him, therefore he is not moved by their talk. (859)

13. 'Free from covetousness, without avarice, the Muni does not reckon himself amongst the distinguished, nor amongst the plain, nor amongst the low, he does not enter time, being delivered from time[1]. (860)

14. 'He for whom there is nothing in the world (which he may call) his own, who does not grieve over what is no more, and

does not walk amongst the Dhammas (after his wish), he is called calm[2].' (861)

Purâbhedasutta is ended.

11. KALAHAVIVÂDASUTTA.

The origin of contentions, disputes, &c. &c.
1. 'Whence (do spring up) contentions and disputes, lamentation and sorrow together with envy;

[1. Vîtagedho amakkharî
Na ussesu vadate muni
Na samesu na omesu,
Kappam n' eti akappiyo.

2. Comp. infra, Attadandasutta, v. 16, and Dhp. v. 367.]

p. 165

and arrogance and conceit together with slander, whence do these spring up? pray, tell me this.' (862)

2. 'From dear (objects) spring up contentions and disputes, lamentation and sorrow together with envy; arrogance and conceit together with slander; contentions and disputes are joined with envy, and there is slander in the disputes arisen.' (863)

3. 'The dear (objects) in the world whence do they originate, and (whence) the covetousness that prevails in the world, and desire and fulfilment whence do they originate, which are (of consequence) for the future state of a man[1]?' (864)

4. 'From wish[2] originate the dear (objects) in the world, and the covetousness that prevails in the world, and desire and fulfilment originate from it, which are (of consequence) for the future state of a man.' (865)

5. 'From what has wish in the world its origin, and resolutions[3] whence do they spring, anger and falsehood and doubt, and the Dhammas which are made known by the Samana (Gotama)?' (866)

6. 'What they call pleasure and displeasure in the world, by that wish springs up; having seen decay and origin in (all) bodies[4], a person forms (his) resolutions in the world. (867)

7. 'Anger and falsehood and doubt, these Dhammas are a couple[5]; let the doubtful learn in the way of knowledge,

knowingly the Dhammas have been proclaimed by the Samana.' (868)

8. 'Pleasure and displeasure, whence have they

[1. Ye samparâyâya narassa honti.

2. Khanda.

3. Vinikkhaya.

4. Rûpesu disvâ vibhavam bhavañ ka.

5. Te pi kodhâdayo dhammâ sâtâsâtadvaye sante eva pahonti uppagganti. Commentator.]

p. 166

their origin, for want of what do these not arise? This notion which (thou mentionest), viz. "decay and origin," tell me from what does this arise.' (869)

9. 'Pleasure and displeasure have their origin from phassa (touch), when there is no touch they do not arise. This notion which (thou mentionest), viz. "decay and origin," this I tell thee has its origin from this.' (870)

10. 'From what has phassa its origin in the world and from what does grasping spring up? For want of what is there no egotism, by the cessation of what do the touches not touch? ' (871)

11. 'On account of name and form the touches (exist), grasping has its origin in wish; by the cessation of wishes there is no egotism, by the cessation of form the touches do not touch.' (872)

12. 'How is one to be constituted that (his) form may cease to exist, and how do joy and pain cease to exist? Tell me this, how it ceases, that we should like to know, such was my mind[1]?' (873)

13. 'Let one not be with a natural consciousness, nor with a mad consciousness, nor without consciousness, nor with (his) consciousness gone; for him who is thus constituted form ceases to exist, for what is called delusion has its origin in consciousness[2].' (?) (874)

14. 'What we have asked thee thou hast explained

[1. Katham sametassa vibhoti rûpam,
Sukham dukham vâpi katham vibhoti,
Etam me pabrûhi, yathâ vibhoti
Tam gâniyâma, iti me mano ahû.

2. Na sannasaññî na visannasaññî
No pi asaññî na vibhûtasaññî
Evam sametassa vibhoti rûpam
Saññânidânâ hi papañkasamkhâ.]

p. 167

unto us; we will ask thee another question, answer us that: Do
not some (who are considered) wise in this world tell us that the
principal (thing) is the purification of the yakkha, or do they
say something different from this[1]?' (875)

15. 'Thus some (who are considered) wise in this world say that
the principal (thing) is the purification of the yakkha; but some
of them say samaya (annihilation), the expert say (that the
highest purity lies) in anupâdisesa (none of the five attributes
remaining)[2]. (876)

16. 'And having known these to be dependent, the investigating
Muni, having known the things we depend upon, and after

knowing them being liberated, does not enter into dispute, the wise (man) does not go to reiterated existence[3].' (877)

Kalahavivâdasutta is ended.

12. KÛLAVIYÛHASUTTA.

A description of disputing philosophers. The different schools of philosophy contradict each other, they proclaim different truths, but the truth is only one. As long as the disputations are going on, so long will there be strife in the world.

1. Abiding by their own views, some (people), having got into contest, assert themselves to be

[1. Comp. Sundarikabhâradvâgasutta, v. 25.

2. Ettâvat' aggam pi vadanti h' eke
Yakkhassa suddhim idha panditâse,
Tesam pun' eke samayam[*] vadanti
Anupâdisese kusalâ vadânâ.

3. Ete ka ñatvâ upanissitâ ti
Ñatvâ munî nissaye so vimamsî
Ñatvâ vimutto na vivâdam eti
Bhavâbhavâya na sameti dhîro.

p. 168

the (only) expert (saying), '(He) who understands this, he knows the Dhamma; he who reviles this, he is not perfect[1].' (878)

2. So having got into contest they dispute: 'The opponent (is) a fool, an ignorant (person),' so they say. Which one of these, pray, is the true doctrine (vâda)? for all these assert themselves (to be the only) expert. (879)

3. He who does not acknowledge an opponent's doctrine (dhamma), he is a fool, a beast, one of poor understanding, all are fools with a very poor understanding; all these abide by their (own) views. (880)

4. They are surely purified by their own view, they are of a pure understanding, expert, thoughtful, amongst them there is no one of poor understanding, their view is quite perfect! (881)

5. I do not say, 'This is the reality,' which fools say mutually to each other; they made their own views the truth, therefore they hold others to be fools. (882)

6. What some say is the truth, the reality, that others say is void, false, so having disagreed they dispute. Why do not the Samanas say one (and the same thing)? (883)

7. For the truth is one, there is not a second, about which one intelligent man might dispute with another intelligent man; (but) they themselves praise different truths, therefore the Samanas do not say one and the same thing)[2]. (884)

[1. Sakam sakam ditthi paribbasânâ
Viggayha nânâ kusalâ vadanti
Yo evam gânâti sa vedi dhammam
Idam patikkosam akevalî so.

2. Ekam hi sakkam na dutîyam atthi
Yasmim pagâno vivade pagânam,
Nânâ te sakkâni sayam thunanti,
Tasmâ na ekam samanâ vadanti.]

p. 169

8. Why do the disputants that assert themselves (to be the only) expert, proclaim different truths? Have many different truths been heard of, or do they (only) follow (their own) reasoning? (885)

9. There are not many different truths in the world, no eternal ones except consciousness; but having reasoned on the (philosophical) views they proclaim a double Dhamma, truth and falsehood[1]. (886)

10. In regard to what has been seen, or heard, virtue and (holy) works, or what has been thought, and on account of these (views) looking (upon others) with contempt, standing in (their) resolutions joyful, they say that the opponent is a fool and an ignorant person[2] (?) (887)

11. Because he holds another (to be) a fool, therefore he calls himself expert, in his own opinion he is one that tells what is propitious, others he blames, so he said[3]. (?) (888)

12. He is full of his overbearing (philosophical) view, mad with pride, thinking himself perfect, he is in his own opinion anointed with the spirit (of genius), for his (philosopbical) view is quite complete. (889)

[1. Na h' evâ sakkâni bahûni nânâ
Aññatra saññâya nikkâni loke,
Takkañ ka ditthisu pakappayitvâ
Sakkam musâ ti dvayadhammam âhu.

272

2. Ditthe sute sîlavate mute vâ
Ete ka nissâya vimânadassî
Vinikkhaye thatvâ pahassamânâ
Bâlo paro akusalo ti kâhu.

3. Yen' eva bâlo ti param dahâti
Tenâtumânam kusalo ti kâha,
Sayam attanâ sa kusalâ vadâno
Aññam vimâneti, tath' eva pâva.]

p. 170

13. If he according to another's report is low, then (he says) the other is also of a low understanding, and if he himself is accomplished and wise, there is not any fool amongst the Samanas[1]. (890)

14. 'Those who preach a doctrine (dhamma) different from this, fall short of purity and are imperfect,' so the Titthiyas say repeatedly, for they are inflamed by passion for their own (philosophical) views. (891)

15. Here they maintain purity, in other doctrines (dhamma) they do not allow purity; so the Titthiyas, entering extensively (upon details), say that in their own way there is something firm. (892)

16. And saying that there is something firm in his own way he holds his opponent to be a fool; thus he himself brings on strife, calling his opponent a fool and impure (asuddhadhamma). (893)

17. Standing in (his) resolution, having himself measured (teachers, &c.), he still more enters into dispute in the world; but having left all resolutions nobody will excite strife in the world[2]. (894)

Kûlaviyûhasutta is ended.

[1. Parassa ke hi vakasâ nihîno
Tumo[*] sahâ hoti nihînapañño,
Atha ke sayam vedagu hoti dhîro
Na koki bâlo samanesû atthi.

2. Vinikkhaye thatvâ sayam pamâya
Uddham so lokasmim vivâdam eti,
Hitvâna sabbâni vinikkhayâni
Na medhakam kurute gantu loke.

*. So pi ten' eva. Commentator. Ved. tva (?).]

13. MAHÂVIYÛHASUTTA.

Philosophers cannot lead to purity, they only praise themselves and stigmatise others. But a Brâhmana has overcome all dispute, he is indifferent to learning, he is appeased.

1. Those who abiding in the (philosophical) views dispute, saying, 'This is the truth,' they all incur blame, and they also obtain praise in this matter. (895)

2. This is little, not enough to (bring about) tranquillity, I say there are two fruits of dispute; having seen this let no one dispute, understanding Khema (i.e. Nibbâna) to be the place where there is no dispute. (896)

3. The opinions that have arisen amongst people, all these the wise man does not embrace; he is independent. Should he who is not pleased with what has been seen and heard resort to dependency[1]? (?) (897)

4. Those who consider virtue the highest of all, say that purity is associated with restraint; having taken upon themselves a (holy) work they serve. Let us learn in this (view), then, his (the Master's) purity; wishing for existence they assert themselves to be the only expert[2]. (898)

5. If he falls off from virtue and (holy) works, he trembles, having missed (his) work; he laments, he

[1. Yâ kâk' imâ sammutiyo puthuggâ
Sabbâ va etâ na upeti vidvâ,
Anûpayo so, upayam kim eyya
Ditthe sute khantim[*] akubbamâno?

2. Sîluttamâ saññamenâhu suddhim,
Vatam samâdâya upatthitâse,
Idh' eva sikkhema ath' assa suddhim,
Bhavûpanîtâ kusalâ vadânâ.

*. So all the MSS.]

p. 172

prays for purity in this world, as one who has lost his caravan or wandered away from his house. (899)

6. Having left virtue and (holy) works altogether, and both wrong and blameless work, not praying for purity or impurity, he wanders abstaining (from both purity and impurity), without

having embraced peace. (900)

7. By means of penance, or anything disliked, or what has been seen, or heard, or thought, going upwards they wail for what is pure, without being free from desire for reiterated existence. (901)

8. For him who wishes (for something there always are) desires[1], and trembling in (the midst of his) plans; he for whom there is no death and no re-birth, how can he tremble or desire anything? (902)

9. What some call the highest Dhamma, that others again call wretched; which one of these, pray, is the true doctrine (vâda)? for all these assert themselves (to be the only) expert. (903)

10. Their own Dhamma they say is perfect, another's Dhamma again they say is wretched; so having disagreed they dispute, they each say their own opinions (are) the truth. (904)

11. If one (becomes) low by another's censure, then there will be no one distinguished amongst the Dhammas; for they all say another's Dhamma (is) low, in their own they say there is something firm[2]. (905)

[1. Gappitâni.

2. Parassa ke vamhayitena hîno
Na koki dhammesu visesi assa,
Puthû hi aññassa vadanti dhammam
Nihînato samhi dalham vadânâ.]

p. 173

12. The worshipping of their own Dhamma is as great as their praise of their own ways; all schools would be in the same case, for their purity is individual[1]. (906)

13. There is nothing about a Brâhmana dependent upon others, nothing amongst the Dhammas which he would embrace after investigation; therefore he has overcome the disputes, for he does not regard any other Dhamma as the best. (907)

14. 'I understand, I see likewise this,' so saying, some by (their philosophical) views return to purity. If he saw purity, what then (has been effected) by another's view? Having conquered they say that purity exists by another[2]. (?) (908)

15. A seeing man will see name and form, and having seen he will understand those (things); let him at pleasure see much or little, for the expert do not say that purity exists by that. (909)

16. A dogmatist is no leader to purity, being guided by prejudiced views, saying that good consists in what he is given to, and saying that purity is there, he saw the thing so[3]. (910)

17. A Brâhmana does not enter time, (or) the

[1. Sadhammapûgâ ka panâ tath' eva
Yathâ pasamsanti sakâyanâni,
Sabbe pavâdâ tath' ivâ bhaveyyum
Suddhi hi nesam pakkattam eva.

2. Gânâmi passâmi tath' eva etam
ditthiyâ eke pakkenti suddhim
Addakkhi ke kim hi tumassa tena
Atisitvâ aññena vadanti suddhim.

3. Nivissavâdî na hi suddhinâyo
Pakappitâ ditthi purekkharâno
Yam nissito tattha subham vadâno
Suddhim vado tattha, tath' addasâ so.]

p. 174

number (of living beings), (he is) no follower of (philosophical) views, nor a friend of knowledge; and having penetrated the opinions that have arisen amongst people, he is indifferent to learning, while others acquire it. (911)

18. The Muni, having done away with ties here in the world, is no partisan in the disputes that have arisen; appeased amongst the unappeased he is indifferent, not embracing learning, while others acquire it. (912)

19. Having abandoned his former passions, not contracting new ones, not wandering according to his wishes, being no dogmatist, he is delivered from the (philosophical) views, being wise, and he does not cling to the world, neither does he blame himself. (913)

20. Being secluded amongst all the doctrines (dhamma), whatever has been seen, heard, or thought, he is a Muni who has laid down his burden and is liberated, not belonging to time (na kappiyo), not dead, not wishing for anything. So said Bhagavat. (914)

Mahâviyûhasutta is ended.

14. TUVATAKASUTTA.

How a Bhikkhu attains bliss, what his duties are, and what he is to avoid.

1. 'I ask thee, who art a kinsman of the Âdikkas and a great Isi, about seclusion (viveka) and the state of peace. How is a Bhikkhu, after having seen it, extinguished, not grasping at anything in the world?' (915)

p. 175

2. 'Let him completely cut off the root of what is called papañka[1] (delusion), thinking "I am wisdom;"'--so said Bhagavat,--'all the desires that arise inwardly, let him learn to subdue them, always being thoughtful. (916)

3. 'Let him learn every Dhamma inwardly or outwardly; let him not therefore be proud, for that is not called bliss by the good. (917)

4. 'Let him not therefore think himself better (than others or) low or equal (to others); questioned by different people, let him not adorn himself[2]. (918)

5. 'Let the Bhikkhu be appeased inwardly, let him not seek peace from any other (quarter); for him who is inwardly appeased there is nothing grasped or rejected. (919)

6. 'As in the middle (i.e. depth) of the sea no wave is born, (but as it) remains still[3], so let the Bhikkhu be still[3], without desire, let him not desire anything whatever.' (920)

7. He with open eyes expounded clearly the Dhamma that removes (all) dangers; tell (now) the religious practices; the precepts or contemplation[4]. (921)

8. Bhagavat: 'Let him not be greedy with his eyes, let him keep his ears from the talk of the town, let him not be greedy after sweet things, and let him not desire anything in the world. (922)

9. 'When he is touched by the touch (of illness),

[1. Aviggâdayo kilesâ. Commentator.

2. Nâtumânam vikappayan titthe.

3. Thito.

4. Akittayi vivatakakkhu sakkhi
Dhammam parissayavinayam,
Patipadam vadehi, bhaddan te,
Pâtimokkham athavâpi samâdhim.]

let the Bhikkhu not lament, and let him not wish for existence anywhere, and let him not tremble at dangers. (923)

10. 'Having obtained boiled rice and drink, solid food and clothes, let him not store up (these things), and let him not be anxious, if he does not get them. (924)

11. 'Let him be meditative, not prying, let him abstain from misbehaviour[1], let him not be indolent, let the Bhikkhu live in his quiet dwelling. (925)

12. 'Let him not sleep too much, let him apply himself ardently to watching, let him abandon sloth, deceit, laughter, sport, sexual intercourse, and adornment. (926)

13. 'Let him not apply himself to practising (the hymns of) the Âthabbana(-veda), to (the interpretation of) sleep and signs, nor to astrology; let not (my) follower (mâmaka) devote himself to (interpreting) the cry of birds, to causing impregnation, nor to (the art of) medicine. (927)

14. 'Let the Bhikkhu not tremble at blame, nor puff himself up

when praised; let him drive off covetousness together with avarice, anger, and slander. (928)

15. 'Let the Bhikkhu not be engaged in purchase and sale, let him not blame others in anything, let him not scold in the village, let him not from love of gain speak to people. (929)

16. 'Let not the Bhikkhu be a boaster, and let him not speak coherent[2] language; let him not learn pride, let him not speak quarrelsome language. (930)

[1. Virame kukkukkam.

2. Payuta; comp. Nâlakasutta, v. 33.]

p. 177

17. 'Let him not be led into falsehood, let him not consciously do wicked things; and with respect to livelihood, understanding, virtue, and (holy) works let him not despise others. (931)

18. 'Having heard much talk from much-talking Samanas let him not irritated answer them with harsh language; for the good do not thwart[1] others. (932)

19. 'Having understood this Dhamma, let the investigating and always thoughtful Bhikkhu learn; having conceived bliss to consist in peace, let him not be indolent in Gotama's commandments. (933)

20. 'For he a conqueror unconquered saw the Dhamma visibly, without any traditional instruction[2]; therefore let him learn, heedful in his, Bhagavat's, commandments, and always worshipping.' (934)

Tuvatakasutta is ended.

15. ATTADANDASUTTA.

Description of an accomplished Muni.
1. From him who has seized a stick fear arises. Look at people killing (each other); I will tell of grief as it is known to me. (935)

2. Seeing people struggling like fish in (a pond with) little water, seeing them obstructed by each other, a fear came over me. (936)

3. The world is completely unsubstantial, all quarters are shaken; wishing for a house for myself I did not see (one)

uninhabited. (937)

4. But having seen (all beings) in the end obstructed, discontent arose in me; then I saw in

[1. Patisenikaronti.

2. Sakkhi dhammam anîtiham adassî.]

p. 178

this world an arrow, difficult to see, stuck in the heart. (938)

5. He who has been pierced by this arrow runs through all quarters; but having drawn out that arrow, he will not run, he will sit down (quietly). (939)

6. There (many) studies are gone through; what is tied in the world let him not apply himself to (untie) it; having wholly transfixed desire, let him learn his own extinction (nibbâna). (940)

7. Let the Muni be truthful, without arrogance, undeceitful, free

from slander, not angry, let him overcome avarice. (941)

8. Let the man who has turned his mind to Nibbâna conquer sleepiness, drowsiness, and sloth; let him not live together with indolence, let him not indulge in conceit. (942)

9. Let him not be led into falsehood, let him not turn his affection to form; let him penetrate arrogance, let him wander abstaining from violence. (943)

10. Let him not delight in what is old, let him not bear with what is new, let him not grieve for what is lost, let him not give himself up to desire[1]. (944)

11. (This desire) I call greed, the great stream, I call (it) precipitation, craving, a trouble, a bog of lust difficult to cross[2]. (945)

12. The Muni who without deviating from truth

[1. Âkâsam na sito siyâ ti tanham nissito na bhaveyya. Commentator.

2. Gedham brûmi mahogho ti
Âgavam brûmi gappanam

287

Ârammanam pakappanam
Kâmapamko durakkayo.]

p. 179

stands fast on the firm ground (of Nibbâna, being) a Brâhmana, he, having forsaken everything, is indeed called calm. (946)

13. He indeed is wise, he is accomplished, having understood the Dhamma independent (of everything); wandering rightly in the world he does not envy any one here. (947)

14. Whosoever has here overcome lust, a tie difficult to do away with in the world, he does not grieve, he does not covet[1], having cut off the stream, and being without bonds. (948)

15. What is before (thee), lay that aside; let there be nothing behind thee; if thou wilt not grasp after what is in the middle, thou wilt wander calm[2]. (949)

16. The man who has no desire at all for name and form (individuality) and who does not grieve over what is no more, he indeed does not decay in the world[3]. (950)

17. He who does not think, 'this is mine' and 'for others there is also something,' he, not having egotism, does not grieve at having nothing[4]. (951)

18. Not being harsh, not greedy, being without desire, and being the same under all circumstances (samo[5]),--that I call a good result, when asked about an undaunted man. (952)

19. For him who is free from desire, for the

[1. Nâggheti = nâbhigghati (read nâbhigghâyati). Commentator.

2. Comp. infra, Gatukannin's question, v. 4, and Dhammapada, p. 308.

3. Comp. infra, Gatukannin's question, v. 5.

4. Yassa n'atthi 'idam me' ti
'Paresam vâpi kiñkanam'
Mamattam so asamvindam
'N' atthi me' ti na sokati.

5. = upekhako. Commentator.]

discerning (man) there is no Samkhâra; abstaining from every
sort of effort he sees happiness everywhere[1]. (953)

20. The Muni does not reckon himself amongst the plain, nor
amongst the low, nor amongst the distinguished; being calm
and free from avarice, he does not grasp after nor reject
anything[2]. (954)

Attadandasutta is ended.

16. SÂRIPUTTASUTTA.

On Sâriputta asking what a Bhikkhu is to devote himself to,
Buddha shows what life he is to lead.
1. 'Neither has before been seen by me,'--so said the venerable
Sâriputta,--'nor has any one heard of such a beautifully-
speaking master, a teacher arrived from the Tusita heaven.
(955)

2. 'As he, the clearly-seeing, appears to the world of men and
gods, after having dispelled all darkness, so he wanders alone in
the midst (of people). (956)

3. 'To this Buddha, who is independent, unchanged, a guileless teacher, who has arrived (in the world), I have come supplicatingly with a question[3] from many who are bound in this world. (957)

4. 'To a Bhikkhu who is loath (of the world) and affects an isolated seat, the root of a tree or a cemetery, or (who lives) in the caves of the mountains, (958)

[1. Anegassa vigânato
N' atthi kâki nisamkhiti,
Virato so viyârambhâ
Khemam passati sabbadhi.

2. Comp. supra, Purâbhedasutta, vv. 15, 20 {sic., vv. 8, 13}.

3. Atthi pañhena âgamim = atthiko pañhena âgato 'mhîti atthikânam vâ pañhena atthi âgamanañ kâ ti. Commentator.]

p. 181

5. 'How many dangers (are there not) in these various dwelling-places at which the Bhikkhu does not tremble in his quiet dwelling! (959)

6. 'How many dangers (are there not) in the world for him who goes to the immortal region[1], (dangers) which the Bhikkhu overcomes in his distant dwelling! (960)

7. 'Which are his words, which are his objects in this world, which are the virtue and (holy) works of the energetic Bhikkhu? (961)

8. 'What study having devoted himself to, intent on one object[2], wise and thoughtful, can he blow off his own filth as the smith (blows off) that of the silver[3]?' (962)

9. 'What is pleasant for him who is disgusted (with birth, &c.), O Sâriputta,'--so said Bhagavat,--'if he cultivates a lonely dwelling-place, and loves perfect enlightenment in accordance with the Dhamma, that I will tell thee as I understand it. (963)

10. 'Let not the wise and thoughtful Bhikkhu wandering on the borders[4] be afraid of the five dangers: gad-flies and (all other) flies[5], snakes, contact with (evil) men[6], and quadrupeds. (964)

11. 'Let him not be afraid of adversaries[7], even having seen many dangers from them; further he

[1. Gakkhato amatam disam.

2. Ekodi = ekaggakitto. Commentator.

3. Comp. Dhp. v. 239.

4. Pariyantakâri.

5. Damsâdhipâtânan ti pingalamakkhikânañ ka sesamakkhikânañ ka, sesamakkhikâ hi tato adhipatitvâ khâdanti, tasmâ adhipâtâ ti vukkanti. Commentator.

6. Manussaphassânan ti korâdiphassânam. Commentator.

7. Paradhammikânam.]

p. 182

will overcome other dangers while seeking what is good. (965)

12. 'Touched by sickness and hunger let him endure cold and excessive heat, let him, touched by them in many ways, and

being houseless, make strong exertions. (966)

13. 'Let him not commit theft, let him not speak falsely, let him touch friendly what is feeble or strong, what he acknowledges to be the agitation of the mind, let him drive that off as a partisan of Kanha (i.e. Mâra). (967)

14. 'Let him not fall into the power of anger and arrogance; having dug up the root of these, let him live, and let him overcome both what is pleasant and what is unpleasant. (968)

15. 'Guided by wisdom, taking delight in what is good, let him scatter those dangers, let him overcome discontent in his distant dwelling, let him overcome the four causes of lamentation. (969)

16. 'What shall I eat, or where shall I eat?--he lay indeed uncomfortably (last night)--where shall I lie this night? let the Sekha who wanders about houseless subdue these lamentable doubts. (970)

17. 'Having had in (due) time both food and clothes, let him know moderation in this world for the sake of happiness; guarded in these (things) and wandering restrained in the village let him, even (if he be) irritated, not speak harsh words. (971)

18. 'Let him be with down-cast eyes, and not prying, devoted to meditation, very watchful; having acquired equanimity let him with a composed mind cut off the seat of doubt, and misbehaviour. (972)

19. 'Urged on by words (of his teachers) let him be thoughtful and rejoice (at this urging), let

p. 183

him break stubbornness in his fellow-students, let him utter propitious words and not unseasonable, let him not think detractingly of others. (973)

20. 'And then the five impurities in the world, the subjection of which he must learn thoughtfully,--let him overcome passion for form, sound and taste, smell and touch. (974)

21. 'Let the Bhikkhu subdue his wish for these Dhammas and be thoughtful, and with his mind well liberated, then in time he will, reflecting upon Dhamma, and having become intent upon one object, destroy darkness.' So said Bhagavat. (975)

Sâriputtasutta is ended.

Atthakavagga, the fourth.

V. PÂRÂYANAVAGGA.

1. VATTHUGÂTHÂ.

To the Brâhmana Bâvarî, living on the banks of the Godhâvarî, in Assaka's territory, comes another Brâhmana and asks for five hundred pieces of money, but not getting them he curses Bâvarî, saying, 'May thy head on the seventh day hence cleave into seven.' A deity comforts Bâvarî by referring him to Buddha. Then Bâvarî sends his sixteen disciples to Buddha, and each of thern asks Buddha a question.

1. From the beautiful city of the Kosalas (Sâvatthî) a Brâhmana, well versed in the hymns, went to the South (Dakkhinâpatha) wishing for nothingness[1]. (976)

2. In Assaka's territory, in the neighbourhood of Alaka, he dwelt on the banks of the Godhâvarî, (living) on gleanings and fruit. (977)

3. And close by the bank there was a large village, with the income of which he prepared a great sacrifice. (978)

4. Having offered the great sacrifice, he again entered the hermitage. Upon his re-entering, another Brâhmana arrived, (979)

5. With swollen feet[2], trembling, covered with mud, with dust on his head. And he going up

[1. Âkiñkañña.

2. Ugghattapâdo ti maggakkamanena ghattapâdatalo panhikâya vâ panhikam gopphakena vâ gopphakam gannukena gannukam âgantvâpi ghattapâdo. Commentator.]

p. 185

to him (i.e. the first Brâhmana) demanded five hundred (pieces of money). (980)

6. Bâvarî, seeing him, bade him be seated, asked him whether he was happy and well, and spoke as follows: (981)

7. 'What gifts I had are all given away by me; pardon me, O Brâhmana, I have no five hundred.' (982)

8. 'If thou wilt not give to me who asks, may thy head on the seventh clay cleave into seven.' (983)

9. So after the usual ceremonies this impostor made known his fearful (curse). On hearing these his words Bâvarî became sorrowful. (984)

10. He wasted away taking no food, transfixed by the arrow of grief, but yet his mind delighted in meditation. (985)

11. Seeing Bâvarî struck with horror and sorrowful, the benevolent deity (of that place) approached him and said as follows: (986)

12. 'He does not know (anything about) the head; he is a hypocrite coveting riches; knowledge of the head and head-splitting is not found in him[1].' (987)

13. 'If the venerable (deity) knows it, then tell me, when asked, all about the head and head-splitting; let us hear thy words.' (988)

14. 'I do not know this; knowledge of it is not found in me; as to the head and head-splitting, this is to be seen by Buddhas

(only).' (989)

15. 'Who then, say, in the circumference of the

[1. Na so muddham pagânâti,
Kuhako so dhanatthiko,
Muddhani muddhapâte ka
Ñânam tassa na viggati.]

p. 186

earth knows the head and head-splitting, tell me that, O deity?'
(990)

16. 'Formerly went out from Kapilavatthu a ruler of the world,
an offspring of the Okkâka king, the Sakya son, the light-giving;
(991)

17. 'He is, O Brâhmana, the perfectly Enlightened (Sambuddha);
perfect in all things, he has attained the power of all knowledge,
sees clearly in everything; he has arrived at the destruction of
all things, and is liberated in the destruction of the upadhis[1].
(992)

18. 'He is Buddha, he is Bhagavat in the world, he, the clearly-

seeing, teaches the Dhamma; go thou to him and ask, he will explain it to thee.' (993)

19. Having heard the word 'Sambuddha,' Bâvarî rejoiced, his grief became little, and he was filled with great delight. (994)

20. Bâvarî glad, rejoicing, and eager asked the deity: 'In what village or in what town or in what province dwells the chief of the world, that going there we may adore the perfectly Enlightened, the first of men?' (995)

21. 'In Sâvatthî, the town of the Kosalas, dwells Gina (the Victorious), of great understanding and excellent wide knowledge, he the Sakya son, unyoked, free from passion, skilled in head-splitting, the bull of men.' (996)

22. Then (Bâvarî) addressed his disciples, Brâhmanas, perfect in the hymns: 'Come, youths, I will tell (you something), listen to my words: (997)

23. 'He whose appearance in the world is difficult to be met with often, he is at the present time[2]

[1. Sabbadhammakkhayam patto (i.e. nibbâna)
Vimutto upadhisamkhaye.

p. 187

born in the world and widely renowned as Sambuddha (the perfectly Enlightened); go quickly to Sâvatthî and behold the best of men.' (998)

24. 'How then can we know, on seeing him, that he is Buddha, O Brâhmana? Tell us who do not know him, by what may we recognise him? (999)

25. 'For in the hymns are to be found the marks of a great man, and thirty-two are disclosed altogether, one by one.' (1000)

26. 'For him on whose limbs these marks of a great man are to be found, there are two ways left, a third does not exist. (1001)

27. 'If he abides in a dwelling, he will subdue this earth without rod (or) sword, he will rule with justice. (1002)

28. 'And if he departs from his dwelling for the wilderness, he becomes the saint, incomparable Sambuddha, who has removed the veil (from the world)[1]. (1003)

29. 'Ask in your mind about my birth and family, my marks, hymns, and my other disciples, the head and head-splitting. (1004)

30. 'If he is Buddha, the clear-sighted, then he will answer by word of mouth the questions you have asked in your mind.' (1005)

31, 32, 33. Having heard Bâvarî's words his disciples, sixteen Brâhmanas, Agita, Tissametteyya, Punnaka, further Mettagû, Dhotaka and Upasîva, and Nanda, further Hemaka, the two Todeyya and Kappa, and the wise Gatukannî, Bhadrâvudha and Udaya, and also the Brâhmana Posâla, and the wise Mogharâgan, and the great Isi Pingiya, (1006-1008)

34. All of them, having each their host (of pupils),

[1. Comp. Lalita-vistara (ed. Calc.), pp. 116, 118.]

p. 188

and being themselves widely renowned throughout the world, thinkers delighting in meditation, wise, scented with the perfume of former (good deeds)[1], (1009)

35. Having saluted Bâvarî and gone round him towards the right, all with matted hair and bearing hides, departed with their faces turned to the north. (1010)

36. To Patitthâna of Alaka first, then to Mâhissatî, and also to Uggenî, Gonaddha, Vedisâ, Vanasavhaya, (1011)

37. And also to Kosambî, Sâketa, and Sâvatthî, the most excellent of cities, to Setavya, Kapilavatthu, and the city of Kusinâra, (1012)

38. And to Pâva, the city of wealth, to Vesâlî, the city of Magadha, to Pâsânaka Ketiya (the Rock Temple), the lovely, the charming. (1013)

39. As he who is athirst (longs for) the cold water, as the merchant (longs for) gain, as he who is plagued by heat (longs for) shade, so in haste they ascended the mountain. (1014)

40. And Bhagavat at that time attended by the assembly of the Bhikkhus taught the Dhamma to the Bhikkhus, and roared like a lion in the forest. (1015)

41. Agita beheld Sambuddha as the shining (sun) without

(burning) rays, as the moon on the fifteenth, having reached her plenitude. (1016)

42. Then observing his limbs and all the marks in their fulness, standing apart, rejoiced, he asked the questions of his mind:-- (1017)

43. 'Tell me about (my master's) birth, tell me about his family together with the marks, tell me about his perfection in the hymns, how many (hymns) does the Brâhmana recite?' (1018)

[1. Pubbavâsanavâsitâ.]

p. 189

44. Bhagavat said: 'One hundred and twenty years (is his) age, and by family he is a Bâvarî; three are his marks on the limbs, and in the three Vedas he is perfect. (1019)

45. 'In the marks and in the Itihâsa together with Nighandu and Ketubha--he recites five hundred--and in his own Dhamma he has reached perfection.' (1020)

46. Agita thought: 'Explain fully the marks of Bâvarî, O thou

best of men, who cuts off desire; let there be no doubt left for us.' (1021)

47. Bhagavat said: 'He covers his face with his tongue, he has a circle of hair between the eye-brows, (his) privy member (is) hidden in a sheath, know this, O young man[1].' (1022)

48. Not hearing him ask anything, but hearing the questions answered, the multitude reflected overjoyed and with joined hands:-- (1023)

49. 'Who, be he a god, or Brahman, or Inda, the husband of Sugâ, asked in his mind those questions, and to whom did that (speech) reply?' (1024)

50. Agita said: 'The head and head-splitting Bâvarî asked about; explain that, O Bhagavat, remove our doubt, O Isi.' (1025)

51. Bhagavat said: 'Ignorance is the head, know this; knowledge cleaves the head, together with belief, thoughtfulness, meditation, determination, and strength.' (1026)

52. Then with great joy having composed himself the young man put his hide on one shoulder,

[1. Mukham givhâya khâdeti,
Unn' assa bhamukantare,
Kosohitam vatthaguyham,
Evam gânâhi mânava.]

p. 190

fell at (Bhagavat's) feet (and saluted him) with his head, (saying): (1027)

53. 'Bâvarî, the Brâhmana, together with his disciples, O thou venerable man, delighted and glad, does homage to thy feet, O thou clearly-seeing.' (1028)

54. Bhagavat said: 'Let Bâvarî, the Brâhmana, be glad together with his disciples! Be thou also glad, live long, O young man! (1029)

55. 'For Bâvarî and for thee, for all there are all (kinds of) doubt; having got an opportunity, ask ye whatever you wish.' (1030)

56. After getting permission from Sambuddha, Agita sitting there with folded hands asked Tathâgata the first question. (1031)

The Vatthugâthâs are ended.

2. AGITAMÂNAVAPUKKHÂ.

1. 'By what is the world shrouded,'--so said the venerable Agita,--'by what does it not shine? What callest thou its pollution, what is its great danger?' (1032)

2. 'With ignorance is the world shrouded, O Agita,'--so said Bhagavat,--'by reason of avarice it does not shine; desire I call its pollution, pain is its great danger.' (1033)

3. 'The streams of desire flow in every direction,'--so said the venerable Agita;--'what dams the streams, say what restrains the streams, by what may the streams be shut off[1]?' (1034)

[1. Comp. Dhp. v. 340.]

p. 191

4. 'Whatever streams there are in the world, O Agita,'--so said Bhagavat,--'thoughtfulness is their dam, thoughtfulness I call the restraint of the streams, by understanding they are shut off.' (1035)

5. 'Both understanding and thoughtfulness,'--so said the venerable Agita,--'and name and shape[1], O venerable man,-- asked about this by me, declare by what is this stopped? ' (1036)

6. Buddha: 'This question which thou hast asked, O Agita, that I will explain to thee; (I will explain to thee) by what name and shape[2] are totally stopped; by the cessation of consciousness this is stopped here.' (1037)

7. Agita: 'Those who have examined (all) Dhammas (i.e. the saints), and those who are disciples, (and those who are) common men here,--when thou art asked about their mode of life, declare it unto me, thou who art wise, O venerable man.' (1038)

8. Buddha: 'Let the Bhikkhu not crave for sensual pleasures, let him be calm in mind, let him wander about skilful in all Dhammas, and thoughtful.' (1039)

Agitamânavapukkhâ is ended.

3. TISSAMETTEYYAMÂNAVAPUKKHÂ.

1. 'Who is contented in the world,'--so said the venerable Tissametteyya,--'who is without commotions? Who after knowing both ends does not stick in the middle, as far as his understanding is

[1. Nâmarûpañ ka.

2. Nâmañ ka rûpañ ka.]

p. 192

concerned? Whom dost thou call a great man? Who has overcome desire in this world?' (1040)

2. 'The Bhikkhu who abstains from sensual pleasures, O Metteyya,'--so said Bhagavat,--'who is free from desire, always thoughtful, happy by reflection, he is without commotions, he after knowing both ends does not stick in the middle, as far as his understanding is concerned; him I call a great man; he has overcame desire in this world.' (1041)

Tissametteyyamânavapukkhâ is ended.

4. PUNNAKAMÂNAVAPUKKHÂ.

1. 'To him who is without desire, who has seen the root (of sin),'--so said the venerable Punnaka,--'I have come supplicatingly with a question: on account of what did the Isis and men, Khattiyas and Brâhmanas, offer sacrifices to the gods abundantly in this world? (about this) I ask thee, O Bhagavat, tell me this.' (1042)

2. 'All these Isis and men, Khattiyas and Brâhmanas, O Punnaka,'--so said Bhagavat,--'who offered sacrifices to the gods abundantly in this world, offered sacrifices, O Punnaka, after reaching old age, wishing for their present condition.' (1043)

3. 'All these Isis and men, Khattiyas and Brâhmanas,'--so said the venerable Punnaka,--'who offered sacrifices to the gods abundantly in this world, did they, O Bhagavat, indefatigable in the way of offering, cross over both birth and old age, O venerable man? I ask thee, O Bhagavat, tell me this.' (1044)

p. 193

4. 'They wished for, praised, desired, abandoned (sensual pleasures), O Punnaka,'--so said Bhagavat,--'they desired sensual pleasures on account of what they reached by them; they, devoted to offering, dyed with the passions of existence, did not cross over birth and old age, so I say.' (1045)

5. 'If they, devoted to offering,'--so said the venerable Punnaka,--'did not by offering cross over birth and old age, O venerable man, who then in the world of gods and men crossed over birth and old age, O venerable man, I ask thee, O Bhagavat, tell me this?' (1046)

6. 'Having considered everything[1] in the world, O Punnaka,'--so said Bhagavat,--'he who is not defeated anywhere in the world, who is calm without the smoke of passions, free from woe, free from desire, he crossed over birth and old age, so I say.' (1041)

Punnakamânavapukkhâ is ended.

5. METTAGÛMÂNAVAPUKKHÂ.

1. 'I ask thee, O Bhagavat, tell me this,'--so said the venerable Mettagû,--'I consider thee accomplished and of a cultivated mind, why are these (creatures), whatsoever they are of many kinds in the world, always subject to pain? (1048)

2. 'Thou mayest well ask me concerning the origin of pain, O Mettagû,'--so said Bhagavat,--

[1. Parovarânîti parâni ka orâni ka parattabhâvasakattabhâvâdîni

312

parâni ka orâni kâ ti vuttam hoti. Commentator.]

'I will explain that to thee in the way I myself know it: originating in the upadhis pains arise, whatsoever they are, of many kinds in the world. (1049)

3. 'He who being ignorant creates upadhi, that fool again undergoes pain; therefore let not the wise man create upadhi, considering (that this is) the birth and origin of pain.' (1050)

4. Mettagû: 'What we have asked thee thou hast explained to us; another (question) I ask thee, answer that, pray: How do the wise cross the stream, birth and old age, and sorrow and lamentation? Explain that thoroughly to me, O Muni, for this thing (dhamma) is well known to thee.' (1051)

5. 'I will explain the Dhamma to thee, O Mettagû,'--so said Bhagavat,--'if a man in the visible world, without any traditional instruction, has understood it, and wanders about thoughtful, he may overcome desire in the world.' (1052)

6. Mettagû: 'And I take a delight in that, in the most excellent Dhamma, O great Isi, which if a man has understood, and he

wanders about thoughtful, he may overcome desire in the world.' (1053)

7. 'Whatsoever thou knowest, O Mettagû,'--so said Bhagavat,--'(of what is) above, below, across, and in the middle, taking no delight and no rest in these things, let thy mind not dwell on existence. (1054)

8. 'Living so, thoughtful, strenuous, let the Bhikkhu wandering about, after abandoning selfishness, birth,

[1. Kittayissâmi te dhammam--Mettagû ti Bhagavâ--
Ditthe dhamme anîtiham
Yam viditvâ sato karam
Tare loke visattikam.]

p. 195

and old age, and sorrow, and lamentation, being a wise man, leave pain in this world.' (1055)

9. Mettagû: 'I delight in these words of the great Isi; well expounded, O Gotama, is (by thee) freedom from upadhi (i.e. Nibbâna). Bhagavat in truth has left pain, for this Dhamma is well known to thee[1]. (1056)

10. 'And those also will certainly leave pain whom thou, O Muni, constantly mayest admonish; therefore I bow down to thee, having come hither, O chief (nâga), may Bhagavat also admonish me constantly.' (1057)

11. Buddha: 'The Brâhmana whom I may acknowledge as accomplished, possessing nothing, not cleaving to the world of lust, he surely has crossed this stream, and he has crossed over to the other shore, free from harshness (akhila), (and) free from doubt. (1058)

12. 'And he is a wise and accomplished man in this world; having abandoned this cleaving to reiterated existence he is without desire, free from woe, free from longing, he has crossed over birth and old age, so I say.' (1059)

Mettagûmânavapukkhâ is ended.

[1. Et' âbhinandâmi vako mahesino
Sukittitam Gotama nûpadhîkam,
Addhâ hi Bhagavâ pahâsi dukkham,
Tathâ hi te vidito esa dhammo.

Sukittitam Gotama nûpadhîkan ti ettha anupadhikan ti nibbânam, tam sandhâya vâ Bhagavantam âlapanto âha

315

sukittitam, &c. Commentator.]

6. DHOTAKAMÂNAVAPUKKHÂ.

1. 'I ask thee, O Bhagavat, tell me this,'--so said the venerable Dhotaka,--'I long for thy word, O great Isi; let one, having listened to thy utterance, learn his own extinction.' (1060)

2. 'Exert thyself then, O Dhotaka,'--so said Bhagavat,--'being wise and thoughtful in this world, let one, having listened to my utterance, learn his own extinction.' (1061)

3. Dhotaka: 'I see in the world of gods and men a Brâhmana wandering about, possessing nothing; therefore I bow down to thee, O thou all-seeing one, free me, O Sakka, from doubts.' (1062)

4. Buddha: 'I shall not go to free any one in the world who is doubtful, O Dhotaka; when thou hast learned the best Dhamma, then thou shalt cross this stream[1].' (1063)

5. Dhotaka: 'Teach (me), O Brâhmana, having compassion (on me), the Dhamma of seclusion (i.e. Nibbâna), that I may

316

understand (it and) that I, without falling into many shapes like the air, may wander calm and independent in this world[2].' (?) (1064)

[1. Nâham gamissâmi pamokanâya
Kathamkathim Dhotaka kañki loke,
Dhammañ ka settham âgânamâno
Evam tuvam ogham imam taresi.

2. Anusâsa brahme karunâyamâno
Vivekadhammam yam aham vigaññam
Yathâham âkâso va avyâpaggamâno[*]
Idh' eva santo asito kareyyam.

*. Nânappakâratam anâpaggamâno. Commentator.]

p. 197

6. 'I will explain to thee peace[1], O Dhotaka,'--so said Bhagavat;--'if a man in the visible world, without any traditional instruction, has understood it, and wanders about thoughtful, he may overcome desire in the world.' (1065)

7. Dhotaka: 'And I take delight in that, the highest peace[2], O great Isi, which if a man has understood, and he wanders about

thoughtful, he may overcome desire in the world.' (1066)

8. 'Whatsoever thou knowest, O Dhotaka,'--so said Bhagavat,--
'(of what is) above, below, across, and in the middle, knowing
this to be a tie in the world, thou must not thirst for reiterated
existence.' (1067)

Dhotakamânavapukkhâ is ended.

7. UPASÎVAMÂNAVAPUKKHÂ.

1. 'Alone, O Sakka; and without assistance I shall not be able to
cross the great stream,'--so said the venerable Upasîva;--'tell me
an object, O thou all-seeing one, by means of which one may
cross this stream.' (1068)

2. 'Having in view nothingness, being thoughtful, O Upasiva,'--
so said Bhagavat,--'by the reflection of nothing existing shalt
thou cross the stream; having abandoned sensual pleasures,
being loath of doubts, thou shalt regard the extinction of desire
(i.e. Nibbâna), both day and night[3].' (1069)

[1. Santim.

2. Santim uttamam.

318

3. Âkiñkaññam pekkhamâno satîmâ--Upasîvâ ti Bhagavâ--
N' atthîti nissâya tarassu ogham,
Kâme pahâya. virato kathâhi
Tanhakkhayam rattamahâbhi passa.]

p. 198

3. Upasîva: 'He whose passion for all sensual pleasures has departed, having resorted to nothingness, after leaving everything else, and being delivered in the highest deliverance by knowledge, will he remain there without proceeding further[1]?' (1070)

4. 'He whose passion for all sensual pleasures has departed, O Upasîva,'--so said Bhagavat,--'having resorted to nothingness after leaving everything else, and being delivered in the highest deliverance by knowledge, he will remain there without proceeding further.' (1071)

5. Upasîva: 'If he remains there without proceeding further for a multitude of years, O thou all-seeing one, (and if) he becomes there tranquil and delivered, will there be consciousness for such a one[2]?' (1072)

6. 'As a flame blown about by the violence of the wind, O Upasîva,'--so said Bhagavat,--'goes out, cannot be reckoned (as existing), even so a Muni, delivered from name and body, disappears, and cannot be reckoned (as existing)[3].' (1073)

7. Upasîva: 'Has he (only) disappeared, or does he not exist (any longer), or is he for ever free

[1. Sabbesu kâmesu yo vîtarâgo
Âkiñkaññam nissito hitva-m-aññam
Saññâvimokhe parame vimutto
Titthe nu so tattha anânuyâyî.

2. Titthe ke so tattha anânuyâyî
Pûgam pi vassânam samantakakkhu
Tatth' eva so sîti siyâ vimutto
Bhavetha viññânam tathâvidhassa?

3. Akkî yathâ vâtavegena khitto
Attham paleti na upeti samkham
Evam munî nâmakâyâ vimutto
Attham paleti na upeti samkham.]

p. 199

from sickness? Explain that thoroughly to me, O Muni, for this

320

Dhamma is well known to thee[1].' (1074)

8. 'For him who has disappeared there is no form, O Upasîva,'--
so said Bhagavat,--'that by which they say he is, exists for him
no longer, when all things (dhamma) have been cut off, all
(kinds of) dispute are also cut off[2].' (1075)

Upasîvamânavapukkhâ is ended.

8. NANDAMÂNAVAPUKKHÂ.

1. 'There are Munis in the world,'--so said the venerable Nanda,-
-'so people say. How is this (understood) by thee? Do they call
him a Muni who is possessed of knowledge or him who is
possessed of life[3]?' (1076)

2. Buddha: 'Not because of (any philosophical) view, nor of
tradition, nor of knowledge, O Nanda, do the expert call (any
one) a Muni; (but) such as wander free from woe, free from
desire, after having secluded themselves, those I call Munis[4].'
(1077)

[1. Atthangato so uda va so n' atthi
Udâhu ve sassatiyâ arogo,
Tam me munî sâdhu viyâkarohi,

321

Tathâ hi te vidito esa dhammo.

2. Atthangatassa na pamânam atthi,
Yena nam vaggu tam tassa n' atthi,
Sabbesu dhammesu samûhatesu
Samûhatâ vâdapathâpi sabbe.

3. Ñâñûpapannam no munim vadanti
Udâhu ve gîviten' ûpapannam?

4. Na ditthiyâ na sutiyâ na ñânena
Muniñ ka Nanda kusalâ vadanti,
Visenikatvâ anighâ nirâsâ
Karanti ye te munayo ti brûmi.]

p. 200

3. 'All these Samanas and Brâhmanas,'--so said the venerable Nanda,--'say that purity comes from (philosophical) views, and from tradition, and from virtue and (holy) works, and in many (other) ways. Did they, in the way in which they lived in the world, cross over birth and old age, O venerable man? I ask thee, O Bhagavat, tell me this.' (1078)

4. 'All these Samanas and Brâhmanas, O Nanda,'--so said Bhagavat,--'say that purity comes from (philosophical) views,

and from tradition, and from virtue and (holy) works, and in many (other) ways; still they did not, in the way in which they lived in the world, cross over birth and old age, so I say.' (1079)

5. 'All these Samanas and Brâhmanas,'--so said the venerable Nanda,--'say that purity comes from (philosophical) views, and from tradition, and from virtue and (holy) works, and in many (other) ways; if thou, O Muni, sayest that such have not crossed the stream, who then in the world of gods and men crossed over birth and old age, O venerable man? I ask thee, O Bhagavat, tell me this.' (1080)

6. 'I do not say that all Samanas and Brâhmanas, O Nanda,'--so said Bhagavat,--'are shrouded by birth and old age; those who, after leaving in this world what has been seen or heard or thought, and all virtue and (holy) works, after leaving everything of various kinds, after penetrating desire, are free from passion, such indeed I call men that have crossed the stream[1].' (1081)

[1. Nâham 'sabbe samanabrâhmanâse
Gâtigarâya nivutâ' ti brûmi,
Ye s' îdha dittham va sutam mutam vâ
Sîlabbatam vâpi pahâya sabbam
Anekarûpam pi pahâya sabbam
Tanham pariññâya anâsavâse
Te ve narâ oghatinnâ ti brûmi.]

7. Nanda: 'I delight in these words of the great Isi; well expounded (by thee), O Gotama, is freedom from upadhi (i.e. Nibbâna); those who, after leaving in this world what has been seen or heard or thought, and all virtue and (holy) works, after leaving everything of various kinds, after penetrating desire, are free from passion, such I call men that have crossed the stream.' (1082)

Nandamânavapukkhâ is ended.

9. HEMAKAMÂNAVAPUKKHA.

1. 'Those who before in another world,'--so said the venerable Hemaka,--'explained to me the doctrine of Gotama, saying, "So it was, so it will be," all that (was only) oral tradition, all that (was only) something that increased (my) doubts[1]. (1083)

2. 'I took no pleasure in that, but tell thou me the Dhamma that destroys desire, O Muni, which if a man has understood, and he wanders about thoughtful, he may cross desire in the world.' (1084)

3. Buddha: 'In this world (much) has been seen,

[1. Ye me pubbe viyâkamsu
Huram Gotamasâsanam
Ikk-âsi iti bhavissati
Sabban tam itihîtiham
Sabban tam takkavaddhanam.]

p. 202

heard, and thought; the destruction of passion and of wish for the dear objects that have been perceived, O Hemaka, is the imperishable state of Nibbâna. (1085)

4. 'Those who, having understood this, are thoughtful, calm, because they have seen the Dhamma, tranquil and divine, such have crossed desire in this world[1].' (1086)

Hemakamânavapukkhâ is ended.

10. TODEYYAMÂNAVAPUKKHÂ.

1. 'He in whom there live no lusts,'--so said the venerable Todeyya,--'to whom there is no desire, and who has overcome doubt, what sort of deliverance is there for him?' (1087)

2. 'He in whom there live no lusts, O Todeyya,'--so said Bhagavat,--'to whom there is no desire, and who has overcome doubt, for him there is no other deliverance.' (1088)

3. Todeyya: 'Is he without breathing or is he breathing, is he possessed of understanding or is he forming himself an understanding[2]? Explain this to me, O thou all-seeing one, that I may know a Muni, O Sakka.' (1089)

[1. Etad aññâya ye satâ
Ditthadhammâbhinibhutâ
Upasantâ ka tedasâ (?)[*]
Tiññâ loke visattikam.

2. Nirâsaso so uda âsasâno
Paññânavâ so uda paññakappî.

*. B reads ye satâ instead of tedasâ.]

p. 203

4. Buddha: 'He is without breathing, he is not breathing, he is possessed of understanding, and he is not forming himself an understanding; know, O Todeyya, that such is the Muni, not

326

possessing anything, not cleaving to lust and existence.' (1090)

Todeyyamânavapukkhâ is ended.

11. KAPPAMÂNAVAPUKKHÂ.

1. 'For those who stand in the middle of the water,'--so said the venerable Kappa,--'in the formidable stream that has set in, for those who are overcome by decay and death, tell me of an island, O venerable man, and tell thou me of an island that this (pain) may not again come on[1].' (1091)

2. 'For those who stand in the middle of the water, O Kappa,'--so said Bhagavat,--'in the formidable stream that has set in, for those overcome by decay and death, I will tell thee of an island, O Kappa.' (1092)

3. 'This matchless island, possessing nothing (and) grasping after nothing, I call Nibbâna, the destruction of decay and death[2]. (1093)

[1. Tvañ ka me dipam[*] akkhâb
Yathâ yidam nâparam siyâ.

2. Akiñkanam anâdânam
Etam dîpam anâpâram
Nibbânam iti nam brûmi
Garâmakkuparikkhayam.

Akiñkanan ti kiñkanapatipakkham, anâdânan ti âdânapatipakkham, kiñkanâdânavûpasaman ti vuttam hoti. Commentator.

*. B reads disam.]

p. 204

4. 'Those who, having understood this, are thoughtful (and) calm, because they have seen the Dhamma, do not fall into the power of Mâra, and are not the companions of Mâra.' (1094)

Kappamânavapukkhâ is ended.

12. GATUKANNIMÂNAVAPUKKHÂ.

1. 'Having heard of a hero free from lust,'--so said the venerable Gatukannin,--'who has crossed the stream, I have come to ask him who is free from lust; tell me the seat of peace, O thou with the born eye (of wisdom), tell me this truly, O Bhagavat. (1095)

2. 'For Bhagavat wanders about after having conquered lust as the hot sun (conquers) the earth by its heat; tell the Dhamma to me who has (only) little understanding, O thou of great understanding, that I may ascertain how to leave in this world birth and decay.' (1096)

3. 'Subdue thy greediness for sensual pleasures, O Gatukannin,'--so said Bhagavat,--'having considered the forsaking of the world as happiness, let there not be anything either grasped after or rejected by thee[1]. (1097)

4. 'What is before thee, lay that aside; let there be nothing behind thee; if thou wilt not grasp after what is in the middle, thou wilt wander calm[2]. (1098)

[1. Kâmesu vinaya gedham,
Nekkhammam datthu khemato
Uggahîtam nirattam vâ
Mâ te viggittha kiñkanam.

2. Comp. supra, Attadandasutta, v. 15.]

p. 205

5. 'For him whose greediness for name and form is wholly gone, O Brâhmana, for him there are no passions by which he might fall into the power of death.' (1099)

Gatukannimânavapukkhâ is ended.

13. BHADRÂVUDHAMÂNAVAPUKKHÂ.

1. 'I entreat the wise (Buddha), the houseless, who cuts off desire,'--so (said) the venerable Bhadrâvudha,--'who is free from commotion, forsakes joy, has crossed the stream, is liberated, and who leaves time behind; having heard the chief's (word), they will go away from here[1]. (1100)

2. 'Different people have come together from the provinces, longing (to hear) thy speech, O hero; do thou expound it thoroughly to them, for this Dhamma is well known to thee.' (1101)

3. 'Let one wholly subdue the desire of grasping (after everything), O Bhadrâvudha,'--so said Bhagavat,--'above, below, across, and in the middle; for whatever they grasp after in the world, just by that Mâra follows the man. (1102)

4. 'Therefore, knowing this, let not the thoughtful Bhikkhu

grasp after anything in all the world, considering as creatures of desire this generation, sticking fast in the realm of death.' (1103)

Bhadrâvudhamânavapukkhâ is ended.

[1. Okamgaham tanhakkhidam anegam
Nandimgaham oghatinnam vimuttam
Kappamgaham abhiyâke sumedham,
Sutvâna nâgassa apanamissanti ito.]

p. 206

14. UDAYAMÂNAVAPUKKHÂ.

1. 'To Buddha who is sitting meditating, free from pollution,'-- so said the venerable Udaya,--'having performed his duty, who is without passion, accomplished in all things (dhamma), I have come with a question; tell me the deliverance by knowledge, the splitting up of ignorance.' (1104)

2. '(It consists in) leaving lust and desire, O Udaya,'--so said Bhagavat,--'and both (kinds of) grief, and driving away sloth, and warding off misbehaviour. (1105)

3. 'The deliverance by knowledge which is purified by equanimity and thoughtfulness and preceded by reasoning on Dhamma I will tell thee, the splitting up of ignorance[1].' (1106)

4. Udaya: 'What is the bond of the world, what is its practice? By the leaving of what is Nibbâna said to be[2]?' (1107)

5. Buddha: 'The world is bound by pleasure, reasoning is its practice; by the leaving of desire Nibbâna is said to be.' (1108)

6. Udaya: 'How does consciousness cease in him that wanders thoughtful? Having come to ask thee, let us hear thy words.' (1109)

[1. Upekhâsatisamsuddham
Dhammatakkapuregavam
Aññâvimokham pabrûmi
Aviggâya pabhedanam.

2. Kim su samyogano loko,
Kim su tassa vikâranâ
Kiss' assa vippahânena
Nibbânam iti vukkati?]

p. 207

7. Buddha: 'For him who both inwardly and outwardly does not delight in sensation, for him who thus wanders thoughtful, consciousness ceases.' (1110)

Udayamânavapukkhâ is ended.

15. POSÂLAMÂNAVAPUKKHÂ.

1. 'He who shows the past (births, &c.),'--so said the venerable Posâla,--'who is without desire and has cut off doubt, to him who is accomplished in all things (dhamma), I have come supplicatingly with a question. (1111)

2. 'O Sakka, I ask about his knowledge who is aware of past shapes, who casts off every corporeal form, and who sees that there exists nothing either internally or externally; how can such a one be led (by anybody)[1]? (1112)

3. 'Tathâgata, knowing all the faces of consciousness, O Posâla,'--so said Bhagavat,--'knows (also) him who stands delivered, devoted to that (object)[2]. (1113)

4. 'Having understood that the bonds of pleasure do not originate in nothingness (?), he sees clearly in

333

[1. Vibhûtarûpasaññissa
Sabbakâyapahâyino
Agghattañ ka bahiddhâ ka
Natthi kiñkîti passato
Ñânam Sakkânupukkhâmi,
Katham neyyo tathâvidho.

2. Viññânatthitiyo sabbâ--Posâlâ ti Bhagavâ--
Abhigânam Tathâgato
Titthantam enam gânâti
Vimuttam tapparâyanam.]

p. 208

this (matter), this (is) the knowledge of a perfect, accomplished
Brâhmana[1].' (1114)

Posâlamânavapukkhâ is ended.

16. MOGHARÂGAMÂNAVAPUKKHÂ

1. 'Twice have I asked Sakka,'--so said the venerable
Mogharâgan,--'but the clearly-seeing has not explained it to me;
if the divine Isi is asked for the third time, he will explain it, so

I have heard. (1115)

2. 'There is this world, the other world, Brahman's world together with the world of the gods; I do not know thy view, the famous Gotama's (view). (1116)

3. 'To this man who sees what is good I have come supplicatingly with a question: How is any one to look upon the world that the king of death may not see him?' (1117)

4. 'Look upon the world as void, O Mogharâgan, being always thoughtful; having destroyed the view of oneself (as really existing), so one may overcome death; the king of death will not see him who thus regards the world[2].' (1118)

Mogharâgamânavapukkhâ is ended.

[1. Âkiñkaññâsambhavam
Nandîsamyoganam iti
Evam evam abhiññâya
Tato tattha vipassati,
Etam ñânam tathamtassa
Brâhmanassa vusîmato.

2. Comp. Dhp. v. 170.]

17. PINGIYAMÂNAVAPUKKHÂ.

1. 'I am old, feeble, colourless,'--so said the venerable Pingiya,--'my eyes are not clear, my hearing is not good; lest I should perish a fool on the way, tell me the Dhamma, that I may know how to leave birth and decay in this world.' (1119)

2. 'Seeing others afflicted by the body, O Pingiya,'--so said Bhagavat,--'(seeing) heedless people suffer in their bodies;--therefore, O Pingiya, shalt thou be heedful, and leave the body behind, that thou mayest never come to exist again.' (1120)

3. Pingiya: 'Four regions, four intermediate regions, above and below, these are the ten regions; there is nothing which has not been seen, heard, or thought by thee, and (is there) anything in the world not understood (by thee)? Tell (me) the Dhamma, that I may know how to leave birth and decay in this world' (1121)

4. 'Seeing men seized with desire, O Pingiya,'--so said Bhagavat,--'tormented and overcome by decay,--therefore thou, O Pingiya, shalt be heedful, and leave desire behind, that thou mayest never come to exist again.' (1122)

Pingiyamânavapukkhâ is ended.

This said Bhagavat, living in Magadha at Pâsânaka Ketiya (the Rock Temple). Sought by sixteen Brâhmanas, the followers (of Bâvarî, and) questioned by each of them in turn, he responded to the questions. If a man, having understood the meaning and tenor of each question, lives according to the Dhamma, then he will go to the further shore of decay and death, for these Dhammas lead to the

p. 209

further shore, and therefore this order of Dhamma was called 'the way to the other shore.'

1, 2. Agita, Tissametteyya, Punnaka and Mettagû, Dhotaka and Upasîva, Nanda and Hemaka, the two Todeyya and Kappa, and the wise Gatukannin, Bhadrâvudha and Udaya, and also the Brâhmana Posâla, and the wise Mogharâgan, and Pingiya the great Isi, (1123, 1124)

3. These went up to Buddha, the Isi of exemplary conduct; asking subtle questions they went up to the supreme Buddha. (1125)

4. Buddha, being asked, responded to their questions truly, and in responding to the questions the Muni delighted the Brâhmanas.(1126)

5. They, having been delighted by the clearly-seeing Buddha, the kinsman of the Âdikkas, devoted themselves to a religious life near the man of excellent understanding. (1127)

6. He who lived according to what had been taught by Buddha (in answer) to each single question, went from this shore to the other shore. (1128)

7. From this shore he went to the other shore entering upon the most excellent way; this way is to lead to the other shore, therefore it is called 'the way to the other shore.' (1129)

8. 'I will proclaim accordingly the way to the further shore,'--so said the venerable Pingiya;--'as he saw it, so he told it; the spotless, the very wise, the passionless, the desireless lord, for what reason should he speak falsely? (1130)

9. 'Well! I will praise the beautiful voice of (Buddha), who is without stain and folly, and who has left behind arrogance and hypocrisy. (1131)

10. 'The darkness-dispelling Buddha, the all-seeing,

p. 211

who thoroughly understands the world[1], has overcome all existences, is free from passion, has left behind all pain, is rightly called (Buddha), he, O Brâhmana, has come to me. (1132)

11. 'As the bird, having left the bush, takes up his abode in the fruitful forest, even so I, having left men of narrow views, have reached the great sea, like the hamsa[2]. (1133)

12. 'Those who before in another world explained the doctrine of Gotama, saying, "So it was, so it will be," all that was only oral tradition, all that was only something that increased my doubts[3]. (1134)

13. 'There is only one abiding dispelling darkness, that is the high-born, the luminous, Gotama of great understanding, Gotama of great wisdom, (1135)

14. 'Who taught me the Dhamma, the instantaneous, the immediate, the destruction of desire, freedom from distress, whose likeness is nowhere[4].' (1136)

15. Bâvarî: 'Canst thou stay away from him even for a moment, O Pingiya, from Gotama of great understanding, from Gotama of great wisdom, (1137)

[1. Lokantagû.

2. Digo yathâ kubbanakam pahâya
Bahupphalam kânanam âvaseyya
Evam p' aham appadasse pahâya
Mahodadhim hamso-r-iv' agghapatto.

3. Ye 'me pubbe viyâkamsu
huram Gotamasâsanam
ikk-âsi iti bhavissati
sabban tam itihîtiham
sabban tam takkavaddhanam.

4. Yo me dhammam adesesi
Sanditthikam akâlikam
Tanhakkhayam anîtikam
Yassa n'atthi upamâ kvaki.]

p. 212

16. 'Who taught thee the Dhamma, the instantaneous, the immediate, the destruction of desire, freedom from distress, whose likeness is nowhere?' (1138)

17. Pingiya: 'I do not stay away from him even for a moment, O Brâhmana, from Gotama of great understanding, from Gotama of great wisdom, (1139)

18. 'Who taught me the Dhamma, the instantaneous, the immediate, the destruction of desire, freedom from distress, whose likeness is nowhere. (1140)

19. 'I see him in my mind and with my eye, vigilant, O Brâhmana, night and day; worshipping I spend the night, therefore I think I do not stay away from him. (1141)

20. 'Belief and joy, mind and thought incline me towards the doctrine of Gotama; whichever way the very wise man goes, the very same I am inclined to[1]. (?) (1142)

21. 'Therefore, as I am worn out and feeble, my body does not go there, but in my thoughts I always go there, for my mind, O Brâhmana, is joined to him. (1143)

22. 'Lying in the mud (of lusts) wriggling, I jumped from island

to island; then I saw the perfectly Enlightened, who has crossed the stream, and is free from passion.' (1144)

23. Bhagavat[2]: 'As Vakkali was delivered by

[1. Saddhâ ka pîti ka mano sati ka
Nâmenti me Gotamasâsanamhâ (?),
Yam yam disam vagati bhûripañño
Sa tena ten' eva nato 'ham asmi.

2. At the conclusion of this (i.e. the preceding) gâthâ, Bhagavat, who stayed at Sâvatthî, when seeing the maturity of the minds of Pingiya and Bâvarî, shed a golden light. Pingiya, who sat picturing Buddha's virtues to Bâvarî, having seen the light, looked round, saying, 'What is this?' And when he saw Bhagavat standing, as it were, before him, he said to the Brâhmana Bâvarî: 'Buddha has come.' The Brâhmana rose from his seat and stood with folded hands. Bhagavat, shedding a light, showed himself to the Brâhmana, and knowing what was beneficial for both, he said this stanza while addressing Pingiya. Commentator.]

p. 213

faith, (as well as) Bhadrâvudha and Âlavi-Gotama, so thou shalt let faith deliver thee, and thou shalt go, O Pingiya, to the further shore of the realm of death[1].' (1145)

24. Pingiya: 'I am highly pleased at hearing the Muni's words; Sambuddha has removed the veil, he is free from harshness, and wise. (1146)

25. 'Having penetrated (all things) concerning the gods, he knows everything of every description; the Master will put an end to all questions of the doubtful that (will) admit (him). (1147)

26. 'To the insuperable, the unchangeable (Nibbâna), whose likeness is nowhere, I shall certainly go; in this (Nibbâna) there will be no doubt (left) for me, so know (me to be) of a dispossessed mind[2].' (1148)

Pârâyanavagga is ended.

Suttanipâta is ended.

[1. Yathâ ahû Vakkali muttasaddho
Bhadrâvudho Âlavi-Gotamo ka
Evam eva tvam pi pamuñkayassu saddham,
Gamissasi tvam Pingiya makkudheyyapâram.

2. Asamhîram asamkuppam

Yassa n' atthi upamâ kvaki
Addhâ gamissâmi, na me 'ttha kamkhâ,
Evam padhârehi avittakittam.]

Made in the USA
Middletown, DE
19 September 2023

38824067R00195